# N. SLADKOV

# A TOPSY-TURVY PLANET,

or,

Paramon's Incredible Tale

of

Travel and Adventure

**Fredonia Books**
**Amsterdam, The Netherlands**

A Topsy-Turvy Planet:
Paramon's Incredible Tale of Travel and Adventure

by
N. Sladkov

ISBN: 1-4101-0782-5

Reprinted from the 1962 edition

Fredonia Books
Amsterdam, The Netherlands
http://www.fredoniabooks.com

# A TOPSY-TURVY PLANET

Perhaps you would like to know how "A Topsy-Turvy Planet" came to be written.

Well, it was this way:

The launching of the first manned spaceship fired all our youngsters with the ambition to be astronauts. And who could blame them! There's such a thrill about the very words—stars, rockets, weightlessness. And the prospect of swimming in air as you do in water, even head down if you so please. And all the surprises sure to be waiting for you on those distant planets—all the extraordinary beasts, and birds, and plants, and landscapes, so different from all that we are accustomed to seeing here on Earth.

But—I reflected—is not our own Earth rich in extraordinary beasts, and birds, and plants, and landscapes! And in the most amazing of adventures, too! Was it not here that Baron Munchausen and Tartarin of Tarascon performed their incredible exploits! And both Munchausen and Tartarin pale before my good friend Paramon, whose stories—and the name Paramon, I would have you know, means Firm and Reliable—whose stories are so fascinating that not even a ticket to the films, not even the most exciting of TV programmes can tear the youngsters away when he gets to talking.

And so I decided to put some of these stories of Paramon's into a book, for all the youngsters to read; because I, too, like Paramon, am convinced that nowhere in creation can you find more beautiful, more amazing, more interesting a planet than our own Earth.

Perhaps it is just that I have never visited outer space, not even in my dreams, that makes me feel that way about it. Or, perhaps, it is simply the deep love I bear to this Earth we live on, to its familiar—and unfamiliar—seas and mountains, forests and plains, birds and beasts. All the books I have written—fifteen of them!—are devoted to Nature as we find her here on Earth. There's one about hunters after bird songs; another about mountain trails that lead no one knows where; a third about what you can see out of the corners of your eyes; a fourth about friendship among birds; a fifth about ten used cartridge cases and the memories each of them holds fresh for the hunter. You'll know these books if you come across them, for their titles reveal their content: "Hunting Bird Songs", "Nameless Trail", "Out of the Corners of Your Eyes", "Bird Friendship", and "Ten Used Cartridges". The remaining ten are of the same type.

So much for my books. As to my own life story, there's no room left for that. Some other time, perhaps.

N. SLADKOV

# CONTENTS

## The Grey Copybook

# NTA

It was the queerest sort of contest! NTA, they called it: No Truth Allowed. The lie-lovers were tickled. And why shouldn't they be? Nothing to do but lie your hardest, and if you outlied all the rest you won the prize. And what a prize! You'd be asked to write a whole book, all about your adventures, and the more amazing, the more incredible, the better. If, of course, they'd really happened. Because the book must be true as truth, not a word of invention. To be truthful, you see, a person has to understand the nature of lies and be able always to distinguish between truth and fiction.

And so, the lie-lovers simply swarmed to the contest. The jury was deluged with entries, some in prose, others in verse.

Manuscripts came in from hunters and fishermen, from hikers and mountain climbers. They came from sailors, from deep-sea divers, from flyers, and even from writers. What could be easier, everyone thought, than to make up a lie? And the prize was so tempting—the chance to tell about all the amazing things that really do happen, on earth, on sea, in air, to hunters, sailors, flyers—those who know at first hand what wonders happen daily on our planet.

The jury—but let me explain, first, what is meant by this word, "jury".

A jury is a group of experts, appointed or elected to determine the winners and award the prizes at all sorts of contests, exhibitions, and the like.

The jury consisted of three members: a chairman and two vice-chairmen. All three were highly respected people, rich in knowledge and in experience. The chairman's name was Fisherson; the first vice-chairman's, Hunterson, and the second vice-chairman's, Sailorson. Who could judge better than they between truth and fiction?

The jury went through all the manuscripts sent in for judgment. The jury picked the victor in the contest. But it was in no hurry to announce its choice. It wanted the boys and girls to hear some of the lies and decide for themselves which liar took the prize. Because it was high time, the jury felt, that the youngsters learned to tell when people were trying to fool them.

And so, the jury picked the three most desperate of the liars and asked them to come and talk to the youngsters and see what came of it.

The liars were only too pleased at the chance to do a little more lying; and the youngsters were pleased too, because they knew how to appreciate a good lie.

Well, then, one day they all got together.

The jury announced that the first speaker would be a liar who had chosen as his motto, "The secret of discovery is, to think nothing impossible."

Not so bad to start off with, the youngsters decided; and they settled down to listen. But first I must explain to you what a motto is. A motto is a short statement of the main idea a person wants to express. Well, then, the main idea the first speaker wanted to express was, that if you want to make discoveries, you must first learn not to think anything on earth impossible.

The story to which this motto was attached was the work of none other than the famous Baron Munchausen—that very same Baron who looked out at his window one day and saw some wild ducks on a near-

by pond. He seized his gun and rushed out of doors, but in his hurry he lost his flint. And those old-time guns, as everybody knows, won't shoot until a spark is struck for them with flint and steel. But the Baron, resourceful as always, clenched his fist and struck his right eye so hard that sparks flew. One of the sparks set off the powder in his gun, the gun went off, and down came ten fat ducks for the Baron's gamebag.

Baron Munchausen lived on an island made of cheese. He had paid two visits to the moon. He had—but there was no end to the list of his amazing adventures.

And now here he was—a slight old man, grey-haired, big-nosed, hurrying out to the front of the platform. Soon his shrill voice sounded through the hall.

"Perhaps you remember, my young friends, the time I struck my eye with my clenched fist so hard that the sparks flew and set off the powder in my gun—a good idea, that!

"But there's no comparing that one little spark with the startling fellow I want to tell you about today. Dynamique, his name is, and he's my closest and therefore most dangerous friend. I never dare shake hands with him.

"If you so much as touch his hand you'll be thrown off your feet by a powerful electric discharge. If he lays his hand on your shoulder, sparks will fly from your eyes, and your hair will stand up on end.

"Dynamique wears on his chest a tin label marked with black lightnings and a skull and crossbones. He got it off the door of a transformer booth. For safety's sake, he never goes anywhere without a fire extinguisher and a fireman's hook. But at heart he's gentle as a dove. And because of his kind heart, when he fell into a river one day and was in danger of drowning, everyone rushed to the rescue. It wasn't so simple, though, to rescue a man like that. The first to hold out a hand to him blazed up like a torch, and had to be put out with the fire extinguisher. The next seized Dynamique by the hair. There was a loud crackle, and the rescuer fell into the water in a rain of sparks and had to be pulled out with the hook.

"Me, though—I never lost my presence of mind. I ran to the druggist's and bought a pair of rubber gloves, and put them on Dynamique's hands, and then I could pull him out of the water safe and sound.

"We've become such friends, now, I've never seen the like. And I don't have to give myself any more black eyes. I just take Dynamique along on my hunting trips, and whenever a spark is needed he touches my gun with his finger, and the gun goes off. No misfires, and no misses. Bang, bang, and there you are."

His story finished, Munchausen turned and left the platform, whistling a piratic ditty as he went, his heels clicking, his spurs jangling.

"Can't be beat," the youngsters said.

Then the chairman announced the second candidate, whose motto was, "All the world looks where I look, but nobody sees what I see."

"Ummm," the youngsters responded dubiously.

A fat little man came forward. He wore a short jacket and baggy white trousers, secured by a broad red sash. A heavy gun hung on each of his shoulders; a huge hunting knife was thrust under his sash; a cartridge box rattled on his belly, and a revolver swung at his side.

"Hurrah!" the youngsters shouted. "It's Tartarin of Tarascon! The great lion hunter!"

Yes, Tartarin it was. The youngsters knew him at a glance. They knew all about his study, back home in Tarascon, hung from floor to ceiling with weapons—carbines, rifles, blunderbuses, Corsican, Catalan, and dagger knives, Malay kreeses, revolvers with spring bayonets, Carib arrows, knuckle-dusters, life-preservers, Hottentot clubs, Mexican lassos, and so on and on—more than anyone could count. And labels everywhere: "Poisoned arrows! Do not touch!" "Loaded! Take care!"

Tartarin was a redoubtable lion killer, as all the youngsters knew. Any one of them could tell you about his first lion hunt. Laying down one gun before him and holding the other ready in both hands, he began to bleat like a goat. Every self-respecting lion hunter takes a goat along when he sets an ambush. The goat's bleating serves to attract the lions. Well, and Tartarin hadn't been able to get hold of a goat, so he did the bleating himself.

Something big and black came in sight. Tartarin fired. A dreadful roar sounded. "Aha!" Tartarin cried, pulling out his knife. But there was no need of a hunting knife. What lay before him was not the dread king of the desert. It was only a harmless ass. And the woman who owned the ass came running up, and gave Tartarin a thrashing, and that was the end of his first lion hunt.

But a hunter's misfortunes are soon forgotten. And here he was now, all ready with some brand-new lion stories. "Lions," he began, "are my weakness. Ah, lions! I need only shut my eyes to see their heavy manes, to hear the thunder of their voices."

His eyes filled with tears. That often happens to hunters, even to the fiercest, in old age.

He blew his nose, and went on:

"Ah, lions! To them have I devoted the best years of my life. I am no coward, but lions—them I fear. Yes—lions, and myself. Because it is only from lions and from myself that I can always expect the most unbelievable tricks. Why, didn't I take it into my head, one day, to eat my dinner in the company of wild lions from the desert?

"No sooner said than done! I had a table set up, and covered with a fine cloth, and a vase of flowers to adorn it. Places were set for the guests, and chairs drawn up. The menu consisted of fruits and vegetables—for the humans, of course—and a zebra for the lions.

"I invited some African friends to join me at table, and then there was nothing more to do but to bring in the lions. That was no trouble at all. I just fired my gun once or twice, and a whole company of lions came running up.

"And so, we sat at table with a company of hungry lions. We ate our fruits, and the lions tore away at the zebra. They didn't seem to notice us—never so much as looked our way. But we—we couldn't tear our eyes away from them! My friends were trembling like leaves in a gale, and the fruits stuck in their throats. Nervous, every one of them. But not me!

"Who could know lions better than I do?

"See these tassels on my fez? Twelve of them! They're cut off lions' tails—man-eating lions. And so far as ordinary lions go, not man-eating, why, some years I've killed my full three hundred and sixty-five of them—a lion a day! And once I killed eighteen in a single night. By morning I was all fenced in with dead lions.

"Well, and aside from lions, I've killed almost fifteen hundred elephants in my day, and something like two thousand buffalos, and as to antelopes, I've lost all count.

"But let's get back to that dinner. As I said, I never took my eyes off the lions, or rather, off their tails. Because who could know better than me the way a lion gives its tail three shakes when it's getting ready to spring. Not two shakes, and not four, but always three. As if it was counting—one, two, three, Go! I know those tails of theirs. I've handled plenty of them. Because I like to catch them that way—by the tail. One grab, and that's that. Only don't ever grab a lion by the end of its tail. It will throw you off like an empty matchbox. The place to grab is where the tail begins. If only you can hold on hard enough, that's the best way there is to catch a lion.

"Well, then, I sat there eating my fruits and watching the lions' tails. But not a single tail so much as jerked. Everything went off peaceably. I could have salted the beasts' tails for them, had I wanted to."

Tartarin hitched up his Turkish trousers and shuffled off the platform.

"There's a liar!" many of the youngsters shouted, highly pleased. "There's the one to write the book of true adventures!"

But those of the youngsters who favoured Munchausen sat in gloomy silence. Some of them even began to limber up their fists, because they felt that the debate would be sure to end in a tussle.

But a new motto was already being read from the platform: "What I shall say is intended not to instruct the listener, but to compel him to think, perhaps even to daydream."

And the third contestant came forward—a fellow-countryman, this time, from Leningrad. His name was Paramon.

The youngsters did not greet him as they had the others. Munchausen and Tartarin were old friends; but this Paramon—who was he? Clearly, the contest was going to be hard-fought, if this stranger thought he could outlie such experts.

"There's sure to be a tussle," said those who had begun to limber up their fists.

Before Paramon could even start his story, question after question came flying up at him, and he had to begin by answering them.

"What's your name?"

"Paramon."

"Profession?"

"Ologist. Geologist, meteorologist, oceanologist, parasitologist, ornithologist, ichthyologist, herpetologist, entomologist, volcanologist, and even stomatologist."

"Height?"

"Five feet eleven in the morning, and five feet seven in the evening."

"Your favourite clothes?"

"Trunks and singlet."

"Your favourite colours?"

"Green and blue—the colours of earth, sky, and sea."

"What do you consider ordinary, and what extraordinary?"

"I'll answer that question later on."

"Which do you prefer—truth or fiction?"

"That question, too, I'll answer later on."

"What do you think possible, and what impossible?"

"Everything is possible, possible is everything;
Everything is possible, of course,
Except the things that simply aren't possible,
And therefore are impossible, of course."

"Not so bad," the youngsters conceded. "Not so bad. We'll hear him out."

"I won't keep you long," Paramon declared. "My story will take exactly sixty-five seconds to tell."

**A Day In the Country.** "One day towards the end of June," Paramon began, "I took a group of young nature-lovers out to the woods, just outside Leningrad. At seven o'clock we watched the sun come up, off in the East. A finch burst into song, the first bird voice to greet the

morning. Then we heard a woodpecker banging away at a cone. Baby orioles cheeped hungrily from their nest in a hollow tree. On a tree stump sat a squirrel, gnawing at a dry mushroom it had brought out from its storehouse. The woods were waking to meet the day.

"The bird cherry was in full bloom, and the air was heavy with its fragrance. Frogs croaked in a nearby swamp, and by the shores of a little lake the pike were splashing loudly, for their time had come to spawn. A hedgehog hurried past us, carrying on its spines a load of luscious apples that it must have found in someone's orchard. Finches flew busily from swamp to nest, bringing ripe red cranberries to feed their young.

"The woods were full of interest. We wandered about all day, watching and noting down all that went on around us. But finally the sun sank westward, and soon disappeared. By the time we got home it was

ten o'clock in the evening, and entirely dark. We were terribly tired and hungry, but highly pleased with our day in the woods."

Paramon bowed and left the platform. We glanced at our watches. His story had occupied exactly sixty-five seconds!

The youngsters did not know what to think.

"No comparison with the Baron's sparks," some of them said.

"No comparison with catching lions by their tails," others added.

It was really a shame. Our own fellow-countryman, and all that, and couldn't think up a decent lie! The sun rose in the East and set in the West; cranberries were red, and hedgehogs had spines. No play of the imagination, nothing out of the ordinary. And not a single lie! And to top it all, the man seemed to be in such a rush—afraid to miss some TV program, maybe. Well, he wouldn't get off so easily as that. First he must come out and answer those unanswered questions.

### Paramon's Reply to Question Six

"What is ordinary, you ask, and what extraordinary? Everything in the world is extraordinary. Take—well, for instance, snow. The most everyday of things to you and me—but for dwellers of the tropics, a thing hardly to be believed. Or take an elephant. A most outlandish creature: it stands ten or eleven feet high, and weighs five tons, and its nose hangs down to the ground! Yet to people in India or Africa elephants are just everyday domestic cattle.

"We call things ordinary when they're what we're used to. But in themselves, are elephants ordinary? Or snow either? Look more closely, and you'll see that there's nothing ordinary about them. Anything may become accustomed, everyday. But nothing can be ordinary, ever. Everything that exists is extraordinary."

### Paramon's Reply to Question Seven

"You ask which I prefer—truth or fiction.

"I prefer fiction. Truth is that which already exists. Fiction is that which will some day come into being.

"I once visited a land of truth-lovers, people who refused to tolerate the slightest play of fancy. What a dull life they led! They never told their children fairy-tales, because fairy-tales were fiction. They shivered all the winter through, and languished in the heat all summer, and never questioned that things must be so, because, as everybody knows, summer is hot and winter cold. They never attempted to turn the course of their rivers, because, as everybody knows, all rivers flow to the sea.

"They had no airplanes, no railways, no vacuum cleaners, no umbrellas, no bicycles, and regarded all talk of such things as idle chatter, because how can a thing be true if it doesn't exist?

"Their doctors treated only bruises, scratches, surface sores. Of internal diseases, they declared, 'We don't see them. Hence, they don't exist.' Their scholars conscientiously registered in huge folios all that they saw in the world about them. They proved beyond all doubt that life and death were one and the same thing. The proof was simple. First they took a live deer, and described it in their learned treatises in full detail: horns, and hoofs, and tail, and head, and body. And then, when the deer died, they examined it again, and looked again into their learned treatises, and found that absolutely nothing had changed, that nothing had been added and nothing taken away from the original horns, and hoofs, and tail, and head, and body. True, the dead deer was not alive; but what, after all, is this thing called life? It is not to be weighed, not to be measured, not to be touched. Hence, it does not exist. Life is a lie. It has never been entered into any inventory.

"These truth-lovers erected no monuments, because people made of marble or of bronze do not exist. They refused to believe that the Earth revolves on its axis. 'Show us that axis,' they demanded.

"And when I said to them that all this truth of theirs was worse than the worst of lies, they threw me out of their country. Ever since, I have always stood for fiction."

"Ah, he can't lie worth a crooked penny," the youngsters thought to themselves. "He's just a bore."

"Show us the winner!" they called impatiently. "Who wins the contest?"

The majority were for Munchausen, but Tartarin also had many supporters. Say what you please, those two could certainly cook up a fine dish of lies! They'd spare nothing and no one, to decorate their tales!

The chairman of the jury rose to speak. The shouters fell still. Every eye was fixed on the platform.

## What the Chairman of the Jury Had to Say

The chairman drank a glass of water, adjusted his spectacles, blew his nose, rustled the papers that lay on the desk before him, and finally spoke.

"My friends," he began, "after due consideration of the contributions made by our esteemed contestants, Munchausen, Tartarin, and Paramon, the jury has arrived at the unanimous decision to award the first prize to our dear fellow-countryman Paramon."

The hall groaned.

"The conditions of our contest," the chairman continued, "demanded above all else that the stories presented contain no truth, that they contain nothing but pure fiction.

"The jury, made up of well-known and esteemed scholars, authoritatively declares that only one of the stories you have just heard is entirely free of truth. And that story is Paramon's. The stories offered us by the other contestants are not fiction at all, but unadulterated truth."

The hall went wild.

The chairman put his hands over his ears and waited for quiet.

When the shouting and stamping ended, he went on.

"The jury has commissioned me," he said, "to make you understand that the story presented by the first contestant, Baron Munchausen, is pure truth, with not a word of fiction in it."

The hall tensed in expectation.

"Long ago," the chairman said, "when people still knew very little, it was easy enough to lie—I beg pardon, I meant to say that it was easy to tell stories. If you so much as hinted that you'd seen cucumbers as tall as a man, or that you'd been off on a visit to the moon, or that you'd heard fishes talking, you'd have been branded to your dying day as a liar and a teller of false tales. But nowadays—nowadays a reputation for lying is not to be gained without real effort. You can't fool people with cucumbers any more. We all know that there are cucumbers in China five feet long. We know that fish are not mute, that every fish emits sounds of one kind or another; that their conversations can be recorded, and even broadcast by radio.

"And as to the moon, that's not so far off either. Our first cosmonaut,

Yuri Gagarin, circled the Earth in 108 minutes; and our second cosmonaut, Herman Titov, circled the Earth seventeen times and a little over—twice the distance from Earth to Moon.

"We have already landed a pennant on the Moon, and photographed the side of the Moon that is never seen from Earth. It will not be long before men are landed on the Moon's surface. I'm not even sure Paramon will have his book of true adventures ready before that happens—so soon may it occur.

"Yes, it's getting harder and harder, as the years go by, to make up real fiction. And that is what our esteemed Baron evidently fails to realise.

"Time was, the very name—Munchausen—was proverbial. To call a person Munchausen was the same as to call him a liar and a teller of tales.

"And that, evidently, is what the Baron was counting on. That is why his new tale so much resembles the old one, we all know, about the sparks he struck from his eye. Only, since that story was written, science hasn't been marking time. It has been steadily adding to our store of knowledge, our understanding of Nature's secrets, great and small. As I have already said, we're not to be surprised any more by a little thing like sparks. And more than that: I won't be the least bit surprised if, some day soon, people begin to consider Munchausen the world's most truthful man. And to call a person Munchausen, then, will be the same as calling him a truthful and interesting narrator. And anyway—can a man possibly think up anything that has never been, anywhere, or that men will not be able to create when the time comes?

"But let us get back to our contest. Baron Munchausen told us here of a man he calls Dynamique, whose hand no one can shake because it's so highly charged with electricity. Well, and what is there so incredible in that? It has long been known that electric charges exist in living beings. The electric catfish and the electric eel kill their prey by means of powerful electric shocks. The electric power of ten thousand eels, a scientist has found, would be sufficient to run a railway train for several minutes. But eels, you may say, are fishes, and the electric eel is equipped with a special electric organ, whereas Baron Munchausen's story is about an ordinary human being. Well, and what of that? There are human beings, too, who in dry weather develop so strong an electric charge that they are dangerous to touch. The physiologist N. Vvedensky has described the case of a citizen of the town of Tomsk with whom, in dry weather, it was impossible to shake hands because of the tremendous discharge, the crackle and sparks, that were sure to follow. Is not this citizen of Tomsk a perfect match to the Baron's Dynamique?

"As you see, there was nothing but truth in Baron Munchausen's story. So that the jury is not to blame. We could not possibly award him first prize."

The chairman gulped down two glasses of water, cleared his throat gruffly, threw a stern glance around the hall from over the tops of his spectacles, and sat down.

### What the First Vice-Chairman Said

A round little man, entirely bald, came trundling forward to the speakers' stand. He was so short, all you could see of him over the top of the stand was a plump little hand, swinging in time to his squeaky little voice.

"I'm an old hunter," he piped. "I'm an old hand at the game. Let me tell you about a queer thing that once happened to me in the woods. I'd shot a bear in its den, and when I dragged it out—good God!—I found the bear had had its hair cut! Yes, all across its side there was a strip of bare skin, with not a hair left on it!

"I thought of goblins, I must admit. But goblins had nothing to do with it. It was all the fault of the wood mice. They'd found the bear lying in their way, so they'd just cut themselves a path across it. Their teeth are sharp enough, no worse than a barber's clippers. So that. . . . But what was I about to tell you? Ah, yes—Tartarin. Well, my dear Tartarin, you haven't managed to lie this time, no indeed. It may sound like goblins at first, yes, but when you get down to it it's nothing but wood mice.

"Take your dinner with the lions. Could a thing like that happen, or could it not? I reply, in all responsibility, that it could. And what makes me so sure? Why, the facts. Myself—ha, ha!—I've never sat at table with lions, true; but there's a well-known African lion hunter who has. John Hunter, his name is. He tells us all about it in his book.

"'We set up a table with a linen cloth and a vase of flowers. . . . Vegetable salad, fruit, and beer were the bill of fare. A zebra was shot and dragged alongside the table. I had it carefully staked down to make sure the lions did not pull it out of focus of the cameras. The three cameramen took their positions in the truck while the rest of the party sat down at the table.

"'I fired my rifle a few times to attract the lions. Shortly, a pride came hurrying along toward us. In a few minutes they were hard at work on the zebra. Now the cinema cameras began to purr. . . . The two meals progressed within a few yards of each other, the lions caring not a whit what we did as long as we left them alone to finish their meal.'

"So there you are—just as Tartarin told it! Why did he try to pass off the truth to us as a lie?

"Yes, it is true that wild lions, nowadays, are often attracted by shots, and come running up in hope of a meal. They are not afraid of automobiles. Often enough, they will follow a car, out of pure curiosity, and when it stops lie down to rest in its shade. Lion shooting has been forbidden, and lions no longer fear humans, nor do humans fear lions.

"We know, too, of a hunter who killed fourteen man-eating lions and cut the tassels from their tails to ornament his hat. His name was Allan Black. And we know of another hunter, Leslie Simpson, who in one year killed three hundred and sixty-five lions—a lion a day. As to Hunter, he once killed eighteen lions from ambush in the course of one night. Also, he killed, in his day, something like fourteen hundred elephants. All this was in the days when the wild beasts of Africa were not yet under protection in special reserves, and themselves not infrequently attacked humans.

"'Be that as it may,' I suppose you are thinking, 'but shooting a lion is one thing, and catching it by its tail is quite another.'

"It certainly is. But let me tell you what Hunter has to say about the Negroes of the Masai tribe, known as Africa's finest hunters.

"'The Masai believe that the bravest act a man can perform is to grab a lion by the tail and hold the animal so that the other warriors can close in with their spears and simis. Any man who performs this feat four times is given the title of "melombuki" and ranks as a captain....

" 'I have seen several of these "tail pullings" during Masai lion hunts and it is a wonder to me that the men attempting the feat ever come out alive.'

"Such are the facts. They are astonishing, but they are facts, and it is in facts that the truth lies.

"That is all I have to tell you, my friends.

"As you can see for yourselves, Tartarin has not earned the prize."

The first vice-chairman waved his hand to the youngsters and returned to his seat.

### What the Second Vice-Chairman Said

The youngsters could only gasp.

Now the second vice-chairman came slowly forward to the speakers' stand. He pushed aside the water jug and began, droning dully through his bushy beard:

"Well, brothers, it's my job to tell you about this fellow Paramon. There's a liar for you! Not a word of truth in all his story! And such a fox, too, blast him! Such a fox!"

The second vice-chairman laughed aloud, but broke off abruptly and looked sternly out over the hall.

"The end of June!" he went on. "The longest days in all the year. In Leningrad, it's the time of the white nights. And he says it was 'entirely dark' at ten o'clock in the evening. Hmph! At that time of the year, in Leningrad, it's light enough at ten in the evening to read a newspaper!"

The second vice-chairman was so aroused that he clenched his fist and showed it to the hall.

"And the sun," he went on. "It doesn't rise in the East, in that season, nor set in the West either. And at seven o'clock in the morning it's away up high in the sky. Who does this Paramon think we are, trying to pull our legs that way?

"Well, and who ever heard of a woodpecker bothering with cones in the month of June? October's the time for that—no earlier. And why should a squirrel eat dry mushrooms from its winter store in June?

As to orioles, they never nest in hollow trees. And the finches are never the first of the birds to sing the morning in. They're always the last. What's the man trying to do—poke fun at us?

"The bird cherry was in full bloom, don't you see, and the pike's time had come to spawn. Ha, ha! In June! A hedgehog carrying ripe apples on its spines, and finches feeding their young with ripe red cranberries. Just listen to that! Finches feed their young on insects, not berries, and neither apples nor cranberries ripen until August or September. Pike spawn in May, and that's when the bird cherrry blooms, too.

"So that, let me tell you, a liar like that Paramon—I'd never let him in at my door! I'd choke him with my own hands, until. ... Ah, but I'm forgetting."

And the second vice-chairman held up a slip of paper, from which he read off the jury's decision:

"The jury congratulates our esteemed fellow-countryman Paramon with his well-earned victory, and awards him the Liar's—beg pardon, the Victor's Certificate."

The second vice-chairman thrust the certificate under Paramon's arm, and pressed his hands so hard that poor Paramon had to screw up his eyes and stand on tiptoe to hide his pain.

The hall went mad. The more pugnacious of the youngsters poked their fists into their neighbours' ribs; but nobody took any notice. Everyone was eager to congratulate Paramon.

Who would have thought it? Lying, it turned out, was not so simple, nor was it simple to distinguish lies from truth. Long live Paramon! Hurrah for the NTA!

## IN THE EDITOR'S OFFICE

Six months flew by. Memories of the liars' contest had begun to fade, when, one fine day, Paramon appeared at the editorial offices and laid a manuscript on the editor's desk.

The editor looked very stern. He picked up the manuscript and weighed it in his hand, glanced briefly at Paramon from under his spectacles, but did not say a word.

The first page of the manuscript carried the title, *A Topsy-Turvy Planet*.

The editor turned the page. On the next page, he read, "Riding Sharkback."

The editor looked up at Paramon again, and said:

"I must remind you that the liars' contest is over. This book is supposed to contain nothing but truth."

"I know that perfectly well," Paramon replied.

"*A Topsy-Turvy Planet*, you call it. Is it a real planet you have in mind?"

"Yes, of course."

"What planet, then?"

"That I won't say."

"Ummm. Well, I suppose you have the right to use your imagination. Planets are like paper"—and the editor flipped the manuscript with his finger. "They'll stand almost anything—as yet."

The manuscript remained on the editor's desk. Here it is for you to read.

# A TOPSY-TURVY
# PLANET

*"The truth is always incredible.
To be believed, it has to be sea-
soned with a dash of fiction."*

> *"But, as we so often observe, real
> life is far more fascinating, more
> extraordinary, than anything our
> imagination is capable of inventing."*

This planet I want to tell you about is a really amazing place. It simply bristles with adventures, one more unbelievable than the other. Things happen there that could not possibly happen anywhere else. Even as a youngster, I was always dreaming about such a planet. I searched for it all my life, through every telescope I got a chance to put my eye to. And one day—at long last!—I found my planet, found it in the very last place I'd have thought of looking for it. I had my knapsack ready in no time, and off I went. The hardest thing, after finding the planet, was to find its doorway, to cross its threshold. Once that was done everything happened of itself, with no help from me. I just threw open the door, crossed the threshold, and—tumbled into the sea.

## RIDING SHARKBACK

I tumbled into the sea and dropped like a stone to the bottom. Not much fun, let me assure you. And even when I got back to the surface again, things were not much better. There was nothing but heaving ocean, all around me.

Not a sign of land, as far as my eye could reach. Not a wisp of smoke from a steamer stack, nor a gleam of white that might be a sail. Nothing

but water, salty and green. A fine start, wasn't it, for my adventures on this long-sought Topsy-Turvy Planet!

After a while I noticed a boat coming towards me, a big boat with a three-cornered black sail. Wasn't I pleased! I swam as fast as I could to meet it. But I soon discovered that my boat was no boat at all. What I had taken for a sail was a huge black fin on the back of a sea monster as long as two telegraph poles set end to end. A shark, it was, and an enormous one, staring straight at me with green, unwinking eyes.

I got my big knife ready and ducked my head under the surface. A gaping mouth was bearing slowly down on me, vast and dark as some sea-cave. Shoals of small striped fish hovered about the cave entrance, going in and out at will. They probably served the monster as a sort of living toothpicks, clearing its mouth of annoying food remnants.

It would be remnants of me they'd be picking out of this same mouth, soon enough, I reflected morosely. My journey was coming to its end before it had had a chance to get really started.

But the shark did not swallow me. It dived before it reached me, and when it came up again I found myself astride its back. I seized firm hold of its black fin, and there I was—sailing across the seas as if I were in a boat.

The shark didn't even seem to notice me. Unhurriedly working its tail, it swam along at the surface, never once diving. Was I awake, or dreaming? Again and again I rubbed my fingers against the stiff fin, or pinched my legs, trying to wake myself.

After a while, for lack of anything better to do, I gave my rusty knife a good whetting against the shark's rough hide.

Towards evening, land came in sight. The shark didn't seem to like the look of it. At any rate, it began to sink slowly under water. I gave it a parting slap on the back and jumped off. I was out of danger now.

Saved—and by whom? By a shark!

Yes, this certainly was a fascinating planet! I resolved to explore it thoroughly.

# CAT KINGDOM

The surf caught me up and landed me on a white sand beach. Not a tree, not a bird, not a beast anywhere in sight. The island seemed bare of life, except for the burrows that pitted the sand everywhere, making it look like a slice of Swiss cheese.

For a moment I was sorry I had left the shark. It might, after all, have brought me to some place a little more like the Promised Land.

But it was too late for regrets. And besides, I was not altogether alone. I had with me a company of tried and tested friends: my two strong arms, my two sharp eyes, and my resourceful brain. And the knife I'd just whetted so thoroughly might come in handy too.

Night drew on. I stretched out on the warm white sand, with a big sea shell for pillow. The stars were sparkling overhead, and through the booming of the surf my sea shell sang me a lullaby.

At midnight I was wakened by a fearful screeching and howling, as if thousands of cats had clinched in battle. The moonlight showed me small black creatures coming up out of the burrows that pitted the beach. Squealing and screeching, tails in air, a wild glitter in their eyes, they all raced to the water's edge, where they set to work to devour the fish left stranded on the beach by the ebbing tide. I lay very still, amazed and frightened. More and more of the green-eyed beasts came pouring out of the burrows. Would there never be an end to them?

All night long the black shadow shapes ran to and fro, and the green eyes glittered, and the howling never ceased. But the sun's first rays, shooting fanwise up over the horizon, found the island once more still and lifeless. All that remained of the night's gambols were innumerable tracks in the sand, from shore to burrows. Round, five-toed, clawless footprints—we all know them well enough: those of the ordinary household cat.

I had landed in a kingdom of cats. There were thousands of cats living on this island. Thousands of cats, and not a single human but me.

I had become monarch over the cats and all their kingdom.


## RAIN


Thunder pealed, and down from the sky fell the first heavy—herring! I ran for shelter. It was raining herrings, pouring herrings, all over my cat island. Soon herring brooks crisscrossed the sand, and herring puddles formed in every hollow.

All the cats came scrambling out of their burrows. They leapt and capered wildly, catching the herrings right in the air. I had the feeling they'd soon start chanting, as children sometimes do, "Rain, rain, come to stay!"

I'd seen many a queer rain in my day, but never before had the sky pelted me with herrings. I wasted no time wondering, however, but quickly followed the cats' example, for I'd had nothing to eat since the day before. The herring turned out to be delicious, and—best of all!—not the least bit salty.

Thunder pealed again, and now it was real, wet rain that came down on the island. The only strange thing was its colour—a bright red. And then the lightning flashed, and the red rain turned milky white. With my own eyes, I saw rivers of milk flowing between banks of clear red jelly.

The weather was getting worse and worse. I was soaked through, and shivering with cold. Luckily for me, there was another change, and the new rain turned out to be dry, so that I was soon warm and comfortable again. Very interesting, this sort of rain: the clouds gather, black and heavy, and release their load of moisture—but not a raindrop reaches the ground. The earth remains hot and dry.

I was quite cheerful again—until suddenly something cold and wet hit my bare neck, and the something turned out to be a baby frog. Again I ran for shelter. Bigger and bigger frogs came pelting down. Green frog puddles formed on the sand, and the frogs' bulging eyes were like bubbles in the water.

In our parts, frogs always croak before a rain. Here, they started their music after the rain was over. Only too glad, I suppose, to be back on earth at last!

Listening to the frogs, I reflected that a good thing to have on this planet would be an umbrella. When it rained frogs you could carry the umbrella as it's meant to be carried, to keep off the rain; and when it started raining herrings you could simply turn your umbrella upside down. Very convenient! Protection from the wet, and your umbrella filled with delicious fresh herrings!


## THE MOST HONEST HONOUR

When I first showed this manuscript to the editor, he asked me:

"Is all this true, or is it what they call—er—the artist's right to use his fancy?"

And he twiddled his fingers questioningly.

"Pure science, every word of it," I answered. "On my honour as a hunter."

The editor doubled over with laughter.

"Your honour as a hunter!" he cried. "Of all things! Your honour as a hunter!"

What about you, youngsters? Do you doubt me too?

In that case, let me remind you once again that all I tell you here is perfectly true. On my honour as a hunter.

## THE FIRST DAY

The unriddling of riddles, the unveiling of secrets, has always been my passion. My heart beat high as I entered the forest. And the wonders began at once.

The tree trunks looming about me were not round. They were rectangular, like squared timbers. They might have been planed by some good carpenter. They hadn't really been planed, of course. They were covered with bark, and carried leafy crowns that rustled softly in the breeze.

With my knife—the one I'd sharpened on the shark's rough hide—I cut down one of the trees. And, sure enough, the rings that marked its age turned out not to be rings at all, but squares. Now, there is a way we have of saying, "the whole year round". A forester I knew told me once that we say this because of the round bands, or rings by which a tree's years are counted. If that is so, then on this Topsy-Turvy Planet the thing to say must be, "the whole year square". Well, it looked as though, this whole year square, I was going to have my fill of riddles!

Coming out of the square-tree grove, I found myself in a spacious glade, with a solitary tree at its centre. I blinked and blinked, and then lay down in the grass and began to count. One solitary tree—yet I counted six thousand trunks! That was a forest of a tree for you!

In the shade of this tree-forest I built myself a shelter of green branches.

In my diary, that evening, I wrote:

"We talk, at home, of seeking shade under a tree. Well, this tree could offer shade to seven thousand of us, if not more."

A wonderful place for a party!


## VARICOLOURED SUNS

Next morning three suns came up from beyond the horizon. One of them was sky-blue, one a darker blue, and the third green. And I'd been planning to lie in the sun and get a coat of tan! A wonderful coat it would be, wouldn't it, if I trusted myself to the mercy of these strange suns! I could just see myself striped sky-blue, darker blue, and green, like a new sort of rainbow.

I wrapped my raincoat tight around me, and pulled the hood far over to protect my eyes.

When I next looked out from under the hood there were eight suns in the sky. Ordinary yellow ones, this time, but eight of them, count and re-count them as I might: one, two, three, four, five, six, seven, eight.

I wasted no time wondering where eight suns could come from. The colour was right, so I started right off on my coat of tan. With eight suns to do the work, I had soon made up for lost time.

I sit here writing this, and I can hardly believe my own words, it's all so very strange. And so I've decided to keep up my diary regularly, and write down everything that happens, because the written word always seems to inspire more confidence than the spoken one. I suppose that must be because, before writing anything down, a person always stops to think—which he doesn't always do in conversation. Once

a thing is down in writing, it has stronger ground to stand on.

When evening came all eight suns sank peacefully, one by one, beyond the horizon. The sunset was bright blue.

## A GREAT DAY

This has been a great day. When I opened my eyes this morning, the first thing I saw was a nose. A perfectly ordinary human nose. It was pointed at me from behind a tree. How my heart began to sing! At last I had met up with living beings!

Then an eye appeared, bright and inquisitive, and then an ear.

Just an ordinary ear, nothing special about it—yet how happy it made me! Clearly, now, there was a human being hiding behind that tree.

I was just about to shout, when something happened that made me bite my tongue. A neck had come in sight from behind the tree. But what a neck! Four or five times the length of mine!

I screwed up my eyes, half afraid to see what would come next from behind that tree. But there was really nothing to be afraid of. Simply, a man came cautiously around to the front of the tree. An ordinary man, with ordinary arms and legs and body. And with an absolutely extraordinary neck.

He was not alone. There were others like him, with just such queer long necks, coming out from behind every tree in sight. And they were all staring at me, curious and half afraid.

I rather wondered what connection there might be between the length of their necks and that of their tempers. But, after all, too long necks were surely less alarming than, say, too big fists.

"Good day," I said to them.

"Don't ail today," they chorussed back.

Well, that was clear enough: "Don't ail," in their tongue, meant the same as "Good day" in ours.

I held out my hand. But they all put forward their noses. It was their custom, not to shake hands, but to rub noses. Well, and why not? I rubbed noses with them, and it didn't do me any harm. And while we were rubbing, I had a good look into their eyes. That is the surest way of judging character. What I saw in their eyes was a mixture of curiosity, pleasure at our encounter, and desire to get acquainted. And that, I suppose was just what they saw in mine. Clearly, there was nothing to worry about in the length of their necks. What did that matter? Was there any law against necks being long?

I was more pleased than I can say. Now, at long last, I would be able to learn all the secrets of this amazing planet. And—best of all—I was no longer alone.

We sat by the river bank, talking away as fast as we could go. Using our hands to help our tongues, we managed to understand each other perfectly. While we talked, my new friends poked about in the bushes until they found three fuzzy spiders, and at once put all the three to work. One of the spiders was set to spin a fishing net, the second—a suit of clothes. Only now did I realise what these people's clothes were made of: spider web—light, fine, glossy, good to look at, and very durable. For the third spider, a frame of sticks was made, which it filled in with a close web of silk. When the web was ready, one of my new acquaintances got out paints and brushes and painted my portrait on it. The brushes were made of the finest bird feathers, and laid the colours on the silk gently, yet confidently. The portrait came out very true to life.

The suit of clothes the second spider had made was presented to me; and with the first spider's net a fine lot of fish was caught in the stream. The fish were amazingly beautiful, glowing with a soft, sky-blue sheen, and the delicious soup that we cooked of them retained this gentle glow.

Deeply touched, I promised myself to repay these good people for their kindness at the first possible opportunity.

We set off through the forest, and a little after nightfall approached the city in which the long-necked people lived.

## CITY SCENES

With the first gleam of daylight I hurried out of doors. I found myself on a broad, stone-paved street, lined on both sides with paper houses. Yes, the houses were made of paper—paper walls, paper doors, paper roofs. Inside, too, the floors were made of paper, and so were the ceilings, and even the staircases.

It was quite a populous place, this paper city. No end of people passing, both men and women. The men all wore short skirts, and the women all wore trousers. Many wore earrings. Not the ordinary rings you and I are used to seeing. These rings were aquariums, every one of them. Real glass aquariums, filled with water, and with live goldfish swimming about in them.

Donkeys trotted spryly down the cobbled street, pulling little carts loaded with cucumbers. Never in my life had I seen such donkeys, or such cucumbers either. Every cucumber was tall as a man; and every donkey wore trousers—two pairs of trousers, in fact: one pair on its forelegs, and one on its hind legs. And all the foreleg trousers were one colour, and all the hind-leg ones another.

I was so surprised, I stopped and stared at those queer donkeys. And the donkeys stared at me. They'd never seen such a queer figure, I suppose, as I must have seemed to them—short-necked as I was, and wearing trousers to boot!

A man came up to me. He had a yoke on his shoulder, and from the yoke hung dozens of tiny cages. I thought at first that he was selling birds. But what he had in his cages turned out to be flies. Huge singing flies.

I walked on, looking eagerly about me. There was so much to see that my neck began to stretch, longer and longer. Another few such sights and I'd become a real long-neck, just like my new friends. All I'd have to do would be to get into a skirt, and no one would see anything strange about me any more.

I turned in at the park. On an open-air stage, a fierce wrestling match was on between a rose and a mignonette. It was not long before the rose, by some skilful flower trick, pinned the mignonette's shoulders to the floor. The mignonette at once began to droop and fade. And the victorious rose, in a crystal vase, was set in the place of honour.

On a big paper house at a street corner I noticed a sign that said, "Dentist". In the doorway stood a man with a whip, and ranged up against the wall stood a long queue of patients—poor suffering souls, every one of them with a swollen cheek bound up in a warm shawl. They seemed very impatient, mooing constantly and pawing the ground with their hoofs. Yes, just as I say—mooing, and pawing the ground with their hoofs. Because the patients were cows. Cows with the toothache, come to see their dentist. Every now and again the door would open and the herdsman would snap his whip, driving in the next patient. What happened inside, I could not see; but when the cows came out at the other door they were much more cheerful, mooing happily and switching their tails. And on their teeth glittered brand-new metal crowns. The local cows, I was told, were so grateful for this care that they yielded enormous amounts of milk.

I got home late that day, loaded with such a weight of new impressions that I stood four inches shorter than in the morning.


## A PAGE FROM MY DIARY

Every day brings new developments.

Here I lie in my paper house, coming slowly to myself after my last adventure. And what an adventure! Had I no witnesses, I'd never dare tell it, for fear I might never be believed again. Fortunately, the witnesses were many.

It all began a week ago, when I made up my mind to climb a nearby mountain. I set out alone. Time after time had I sworn to myself never again to go alone to places dangerous or unexplored. All the trouble and unpleasantness I'd suffered in my life on account of this foolish habit! Yet off I was again, all my good resolutions forgotten.

The climb was easy, and I was soon at the mountain top. The view was wonderful. Forests everywhere, stretching as far as the eye could see.

I was so pleased, I did a hop-skip-jump. And sprained my ankle. Clever of me, wasn't it?

Looking down, I could see the town where the long-necks lived, at the foot of the neighbouring mountain. But the people in the town, of course, could not see me.

I couldn't walk. I had no food or drink with me. No one knew where I had gone. That's what comes of breaking your own good resolutions.

It seemed but an arm's reach from one mountain to the other. But what was the good? Mountains, as we know, can't move.

As this thought flashed through my mind, what do you think happened? My mountain shivered, and stirred, and shifted from its place. My hair stood up on end, I was so startled.

Slowly, but surely, my mountain moved closer and closer to its neighbour. And with it I, too, came nearer and nearer home.

A full week, this ride on the mountain top continued. And all week my hair remained on end.

When the week ended, the two mountains stood side by side. They had met. They had come together.

Wildly, I waved my yellow shorts. The townspeople noticed my signals and came to the rescue.

They brought me safely down. All ended well. And here I lie, resting after a hearty dinner.

I've learned my lesson now. Never again will I make off all alone for places I don't know. I must find myself a companion, a friend I can rely on. That should not be difficult. If mountains can meet, as they do here, why shouldn't people?

# A WHITE BLACK RAVEN

The first bird I saw here was a white black raven. White, I say, because it was really white, white all over: body, and wings, and tail, and beak. Yet it was a raven, and ravens are always black. The very word, "raven", has become a synonym for blackness. Even in songs, you'll hear lines like, "Night-black raven, do not hover...."

There they hovered in the sky above us—snow-white ravens, cawing dismally. What new wonders did they herald? Many! And all of a kind!

White creatures turned up everywhere we went. White jackdaws, white crows, white sparrows, white eagles; a white tiger, a white wolf, a white lynx, a white mole; and even a white black grouse.

On the lake shore, white frogs were croaking.

In the lake, white water snakes swam to and fro.

Both frogs and snakes had pink eyes, and their bodies were so transparent, you could see their insides. A white frog, with a red heart beating inside it!

White birds, white beasts, white reptiles.

I thought for a while I had gone colour-blind!

# UNDERGROUND FLOWERS

Back home, I had loved to wander through the meadows, gathering flowers.

Beautiful things, flowers, and everything about them is poetic. Their very pollination is the work of the fragrant breezes, and the pretty butterflies, and the industrious bees.

On this new planet, there seemed to be no flowers in the meadows. That troubled me, and I began searching high and low. In the end, I found what I had been seeking, found my beloved flowers. Where? Why, underground!

I dug myself up a huge bouquet of underground blossoms. How beautiful they were! Now they would seem pale pink, now a glowing red, now a soft violet. I was very pleased.

Setting out for a walk, now, I always take along a spade to dig myself some flowers with.

What I couldn't understand at first was how the flowers ever got pollinated, underground. There are no breezes down there, no butterflies, no bees. Could it be that these amazing blossoms simply faded and died, yielding no seed? That was a problem that took a lot of thought to settle. But I did settle it, finally.

For lack, underground, of wind, and butterflies, and bees, the flowers must clearly be pollinated by earthworms. Yes, earthworms, carrying from blossom to blossom a fragrant load of pollen.

"The earthworms hovered o'er the blooms," I declaimed.

But, somehow, it didn't sound at all poetic. Facts are facts, however, and there's nothing we can do about it.

## SINGING SNAILS

Bird-lovers the world over never tire of praising their pretty songsters. Tastes differ, however. The people here prefer singing snails. I keep snails, too, in a cage in my room. They are as colourful as birds, and they sing delightfully.

The snail I have just now sings only when it is raining out of doors and I have to stay at home. That is very convenient, because its sweet singing drives away all painful thoughts.

Birds are different. They sing when the sun is shining, and fall still when it rains. Well, and who cares for their singing when the sun is shining? In sunny weather there's no need to stay at home, and no painful thoughts to drive away.

And that is why I prefer singing snails to songbirds or cicadas. My pretty snails sing to me when storm clouds hide the sun.

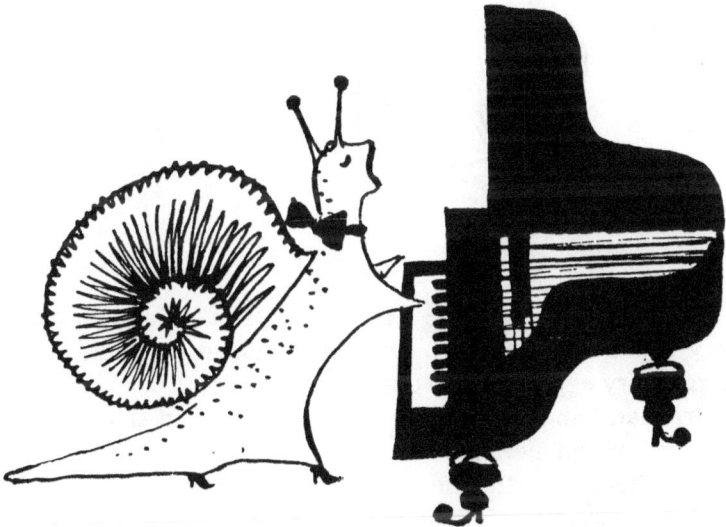

# THE SPECKLED HEN

Everyone knows the old tale about the speckled hen that laid the golden egg.

I can tell you another tale about a speckled hen. Only my tale is true.

Once upon a time there were an old grandad and an old grandma, and they had a speckled hen. And the speckled hen laid them an egg. Not an ordinary egg. A double one.

Grandad banged and banged at the egg, and the egg broke. Inside it lay another, smaller egg.

And then, as in the old tale, a little mouse ran by, and flicked its tail. And the second egg fell down and broke.

Grandad and Grandma were very much upset. But the speckled hen said:

"Cluck-cluck! Don't you cry, Grandma. Don't you cry, Grandad. I'll lay you another egg. Not a double egg. A triple one."

And—no sooner said than done—in another minute, there lay a triple egg.

And that was the end of that.

Who says it's only a story? Who says it isn't true? There the egg lies in the nest, for all to see. Not an ordinary egg. A triple one.

## SCARE-FEATHERS

Today my new friends showed me their poultry farm. They keep so many different sorts of fowl, there's no counting them!

Once a year a harvest of feathers is gathered, for which purpose all the birds are plucked. No, not in the vulgar way, by hand. A special plucking technique has been devised, the technique of fright. When the birds are properly frightened, the feathers begin to fly as if someone were shaking out a torn pillow.

It's simple enough. The attendant beats out a dusty sack against the wiring of the coop, and the birds are so frightened by the din that they lose all their plumage. Then the feathers are gathered into this same sack, inasmuch as the beating has left it clean.

The cocks, however, are not so easily managed as the hens. That is because of the great length of their tails. The cocks have to be kept in

special coops, two stories high. When they roost on their perches, up at the top, their tails reach to the ground.

Such a cock is not easily frightened, and its tail feathers have to be plucked by hand. They are used on hats—one feather to a dozen hats.

All the local people wear feathers in their hats, and sleep on pillows and feather beds stuffed with scare-feathers.

## POACHING FOR FROGS

Poachers—what harm they bring to fields and woods!

The poacher shoots bird and beast in forbidden seasons and forbidden

places. The poacher does not love the forest; and the forest does not love the poacher.

The other day I—yes, I!—became a poacher.

"Fluff and feathers," my friends called after me when I set out, gun in hand, for the nearby swamp. I shrugged. What did I want with fluff or feathers, when all I was after was a new frog for my collection?

And so, gun in hand, I strode along the edge of the swamp. Yes, with gun, not stick, in hand. A stick would have done me very little good in this swamp. The frogs here are the size of chickens. And the way they bellow—like very bulls! You can hear them two miles off, and the sound is enough to give anyone the shivers.

So that it was only with my gun that I could venture on a frog hunt here.

I'd shot all sorts of game in my day—game that ran, and game that swam, and game that flew. But never before had I sought to shoot game that hopped.

Luck was with me.

In hardly more than an hour my gamebag was full.

And then I bumped into one of the local people.

"Fond of frog-legs, eh?" he asked innocently, eyeing my trophies.

Proudly, I displayed the heavy bag.

"You're fined for poaching!" he roared at me, stretching his long neck till it was longer still.

I could only gasp.

Frogs were not mere frogs in this country, I discovered, but game of the first category, like swans or capercaillie in our parts. They are under

protection of the game laws, and may be shot only in the official season.

Thus did I forfeit my reputation as an honest sportsman, to become a poacher. A frog poacher!

What could be more unfortunate?


## MY NEW HOUSE


I got sick and tired of living in a paper house—it seemed so very flimsy! And so I've moved into a house made of clay. It was built for me by ants. All clay houses here are built by ants.

This is what I call a real house. Two storeys high, by our home standards, and with thick, strong walls. A house to feel safe in.

There was one thing, at first, that bothered me. The house had neither doors nor windows, and it was dark as a dungeon inside. But my friends were very helpful, taking all the problems of interior decoration out of my hands. First of all, they cut me a door. And then they brought a toadstool to stand on my table. There's no end of these toadstools, out in the woods. A round cap on a straight stalk—perfectly ordinary toadstools; only they're luminescent, and so much so that you can read by their light.

Also, just in case, my friends supplied me with some excellent candles. Not wax, though, nor tallow either. These candles were made of fish. You simply catch the right kind of fish, draw a wick through it, and there you are—fix the tail into a candlestick, put a match to the wick, and sit down to a book. When you feel sleepy, you need only throw open the cage, and your singing snail will blow out all your lights.

There's nothing to disturb my sleep—no mice, no flies. To keep the house free of rats and mice, I've been given a big boa, very handsome and affectionate. All the people here keep boas in their houses, rather than cats. Another gift has been an array of potted plants, of a kind cultivated in these parts not for their blossoms or fragrance, but as convenient insectivores. These plants trap flies and mosquitoes, swallow them whole, and afterwards eject the legs and wings.

I've also been given a watchdog, to guard the house. I feed my new dog nothing but fruit. It's a strict vegetarian: no meat, no bones. Not much help in hunting—too slow on its feet; but I wish you could see the way it flies! Because, you see, it has wings.

A good-humoured creature, this dog of mine. Neither barks nor bites. By night it hovers about over the roof. By day, it hangs head down in the doorway. Neither barks nor bites—but the finest bogy I've ever seen. The very look of it is enough to scare off burglars.

# THE CRANE-HERD

Nowhere have I come across so many different kinds of herdsmen as here. The other day I saw one herding cranes. And didn't I stare! Talk about swineherds, running after their pigs with nothing but a stick, or

maybe a whip, to work with! The crane-herd didn't run. He flew. In a plane.

He soared high above the clouds, like a swift silver arrow. And before him flew the cranes—long-beaked, long-necked, long-legged.

Only twice a year does he herd his flock: in spring and autumn.

When the cranes start southward in the autumn, the herder gets into his plane and follows them, to protect them against eagles, hawks, and poachers.

Honest folk, hearing the birds' parting cries, look up at the sky and think to themselves, "There go the cranes and their herder. It's time

we put our stoves in order." As to the poachers, they hide away in the bushes.

When winter ends the crane-herd joins his flock again and escorts it northward, back to its summer home. And again the poachers cower and hide, while honest folk rejoice at the return of cranes and spring.

Year after year the cycle is repeated.

Year after year the cranes fly in the lead, and their herder follows close behind.

## WOODEN COWS

Herdsmen have no easy job, particularly cattle herders. Cattle require constant watching, to keep them from straying and to protect them against wolves, and bears, and all sorts of other dangers. Not a minute's peace for the herder, all the long day through.

Not here, though. On this Topsy-Turvy Planet the herdsman's job is easy as pie. Because the cows here are made of wood.

The people are very fond of milk, and so they breed whole groves of cows—beg pardon, whole herds of trees—ah, I seem to be all mixed up. And how could a person help getting mixed, watching the milkmen carry the pails to the woods instead of the pastures and milk trees instead of cows?

The cow trees yield milk the whole year round, at any time of the day or night. And their milk is always good.

It's the easiest thing in the world to herd such wooden cattle.

The cow trees never run away. They never bellow. They never have to be driven to water. They need no protection against wolves or bears. True, they are sometimes attacked by insect pests; but against those the herder has a trusty helper. Herd dogs, you ask? No, indeed. Birds. Because they live on insects.

Yes, it's an easy life—the herdsman's. Nothing to do but lie in the shade of your herd and play away on your pipe.

# BIRD MILK

They can offer you anything, the people of this amazing land. Even bird milk.

Yes, bird milk. I've seen it with my own eyes. It's rather thicker than cow's milk. About the consistency of good sour cream.

Nobody drinks it. Why should they, when they've got tree milk in plenty—not to speak of rabbit milk, which is far more nourishing than cow's milk; or of seal milk, twice as nourishing as rabbit milk. Well, and best of all, particularly for the old and the ailing, is whale milk. A whale yields two hundred litres of excellent milk a day, twelve times as rich in fat as cow's milk.

So that, as you see, there's no need for these people to drink bird milk. It's just their innocent way of showing off, so that newcomers will understand how well supplied they are with everything anyone could possibly want or need.

## A SINECURE

It's an easy job detectives have, on this planet.

Because, you see, the burglars are most obliging.

In other lands, burglars burgle, and the burgled cry for the guards. On this planet things work out differently.

Burglars, say, have got into a shop by night. They promptly begin to burgle, stuffing all they can find into sacks or suitcases.

Then, when all is ready, they hoist their spoils onto their shoulders and—begin to shout for the guards!

They shout so loud, so frantically, that even the pampered local detectives finally wake up and stroll unhurriedly to the alarm. By the time they arrive, a crowd of curiosity seekers has generally gathered outside the door.

Weeping and wailing, the burglars bang at the door from within, imploring the detectives to waste no time.

The watchman unlocks the door. The detectives step inside. And the burglars throw their arms around the detectives' necks, begging to be taken to jail as fast as possible.

Lazily, the detectives set off down the street for the jail. The burglars follow close at their heels.

The watchman locks the shop door, and the crowd melts away, a smile on every face.

The detectives are getting much too fat, they've so little work to do. Such obliging burglars!

## INCENDIARY

I was invited to court today, to attend the trial of an incendiary.

For many years, this horrible criminal had been setting fire to the forests. And never once had he been caught.

The detectives had run around like mad, setting ambushes, following false trails, suspecting everyone—even themselves. But all to no effect.

Summer after summer, forest fires had worked fearful havoc. In the end the population had got so angry with the useless detectives that they had discharged them to a man, and set to work themselves. And then, of course, the villain had been caught red-handed.

The courtroom was full to capacity.

"The Court is coming. Please rise!"

The accused was carried into the room.

Yes, carried. The accused had been set into an earthenware pot. Small, handsome, delicate, the accused filled the air with a delicious fragrance.

Because the accused was a flower, an ordinary flower. For years, unsuspected, it had been setting fires that laid waste vast stretches of forest.

The Court condemned the flower and all its race to extermination by weeding. The country's children were called upon to root out the incendiary.

The audience whistled as one man. That is the local way of expressing approval.

## BIRDHOUSE SEEDS

If you plant a watermelon seed, what will grow out of it? Watermelons.

And if you plant the seed of an ordinary gourd, what will grow out of that?

Well, it all depends. If you plant it back at home, in our parts, the answer is: gourds. But out here things are different, and the things that grows out of a gourd seed are no more and no less than birdhouses.

Yes, genuine birdhouses, the kind people hang on trees for birds to nest in.

In every vegetable garden several beds are reserved for growing birdhouses. In early spring, as soon as the snow has melted, the beds are spaded up and the gourd seeds planted. Soon the first green sprouts ap-

pear. The youngsters water the beds well and pull out every weed. The sprouts grow steadily. Stalks appear, and leaves, and finally blossoms. And as soon as the blossoms fall their place is taken by birdhouses— tiny birdhouses, no bigger than a matchbox.

The sun shines down on them. The rains give them to drink. And the birdhouses grow and grow, until, one day, they are completely ripe— big, and firm, and shapely. It remains only to gather them.

All this being so, it is only natural that there are birdhouses on almost every tree, and therefore great numbers of birds, and therefore very few insect pests to harm the crops.

Anyone who won't believe that birdhouses can grow in garden beds is very welcome to come and visit me. I've a full knapsack of bird-house seeds at home, and you can have them for the asking. Take all you please, and plant them in your garden. If you water them well, they'll grow into birdhouses, never you doubt it.


### DUCKSHOT

I'm an old sportsman, not easily surprised. But, the other day, my neighbour did surprise me.

"Good morning, neighbour," I said to him. "And where are you off to?"

"The lake."

"What after?"

"Duckshot."

I was too taken aback to say a word; and while I stood there wondering what it meant to go out to the lake after shot, my neighbour disappeared.

This morning he set out again after shot, and this time I got him to take me along.

He carried neither gun nor gamebag. Nothing but a wicker basket, and in the basket a live wild duck.

"You use shot to kill ducks," he said. "Well, and I use a duck to get shot."

"Oh," I returned. "You mean, instead of shooting ducks with shot, you shoot shot with ducks?"

"Not quite," he answered. "I use the duck as a decoy. I put it in the water, and hide in a little shelter in the bushes. The duck begins to quack, and very soon the shot comes raining down."

How strange, I thought. Why should the poor duck want to bring shot raining down?

Well, we soon reached the lake shore. We put the duck in the water, and hid in the little shelter in the bushes. The duck splashed about a while, and then began to quack. And at once the drakes began to gather.

"Well, where's your shot?" I whispered to my neighbour. "I can see nothing but drakes."

"Sssh!" he returned. "What are drakes but shot?"

Suddenly he sprang out of the shelter and hurled a stick at the drakes. Two of them fell.

"There!" he cried. "A dozen drakes at one blow!"

There was a sportsman for you, I reflected. Killed two drakes, and called them twelve!

But my neighbour picked up the two drakes he had killed and gave them a good shaking. And didn't the shot come raining out from their open bills!

He collected the shot, weighed it in his hand, and said:

"Ten good charges. And that means ten ducks. Which, added to the two I've got already, makes it twelve. Twelve at one blow!"

I could only gape. I'm an old sportsman myself, but—as the saying goes—live and learn!


## DIGGING FOR FISH

Where do you go if you want to catch some fish, and what do you take with you? You go to the river, of course, or the pond and you take along a fishing rod.

Some of the local anglers called for me one morning. Each of them carried a spade over his shoulder—in place of a rod, you see—and a sack instead of a landing net.

"Come dig for fish with us," they said. "The time's just right. The rivers are all dried up with the heat. You could go bicycling across them."

I didn't wait to be asked twice. I only stopped a minute to get my spade.

When we got to the river, there wasn't a drop of water in it. The river bottom was stone dry, and fissured with the heat. And as to fish! Why, there wasn't enough moisture to keep a frog alive! But those angler friends of mine scattered up and down the river bed and set to work, banging away at the dry soil just as we at home bang at the river ice when we want to drive a hole through to the water.

We banged until we got so tired we had to sit down and rest. And then we banged some more. And then, all at once, someone raised a shout. Had he hooked something, I wondered, on his spade?

He had. He was dragging his catch out from under the ground. A fine fish, for all it was so stiff with mud. And how it jerked, and hissed, and bared its teeth!

Things went better now. Soon we had a whole sackful of splendid fish. We thought of cooking a soup, but there was no water, so we had to eat our fish fried. It was delicious, too, no worse than the fish you catch in water.

## MERRY RICE

The people here have been having trouble with their crops, particularly with the rice. A capricious crop, that.

For your rice to grow properly, you have to give it just the right amount of water, and at just the right time—more of it one day, and less another.

In the daytime, greedy birds flock to the fields to feed.

By night, wild boars trample the growing plants.

Not a moment's peace did the poor husbandmen get this season, by night or by day.

Songs and laughter ceased in the countryside. And in the mournful silence the rice stopped growing altogether.

That gave me an idea as to how I might help my friends. First of all, I asked them to pick me out a band of bad musicians—the worst that could be found.

I got myself a wooden ruler, in place of the baton a real conductor uses, and led my band out to the fields. We struck up a brisk march tune. The musicians played badly, and I conducted worse, but in any case we made plenty of noise. And that was the main thing I was after. We kept up this din for six days and six nights.

On the seventh day the people in the nearby villages began to complain of earache.

I only smiled at their complaints. Their ears, I knew, were not the only sufferers. Every weed in the rice fields lay dead, killed by our music.

As to the rice itself, I measured it with my ruler and found that it had made noticeable progress. Unquestionably, its growth had been stimulated by the music we had been treating it to. Jolly rice, that!

"I'll make it grow sky-high!" I cried excitedly, flourishing my ruler. And the band broke into a lively dance tune.

The villagers began to dance. Happy songs and laughter sounded over the fields.

And the greater the merriment, the louder the music—the faster the weeds all died, and the better the rice plants grew.

The greedy birds were so frightened, they flew off to the woods; nor did the wild boars dare show themselves in the fields.

The villagers reaped a bumper harvest.

It's a long time, now, since the last of the rice was reaped, but to this day the villages ring with songs and laughter.

That, I suppose, is because all the granaries are full of merry, music-loving rice.

So that I have been able at last to repay my new-found friends some little of all the kindness they have shown me.

## CUMBERSOME MONEY

I had the most miserable luck today: I found some money. Someone had lost it, and I had the bad luck to find it.

It's an awful thing, out here, to find money that doesn't belong to you. Once you've found it, it's your duty as an honest citizen to return it to its owner. But how are you going to return it, if you can't even lift it off the ground?

It was only one coin. A kopek. The reason I found it was, I stumbled against it—almost broke my leg, in fact. I tried to lift the thing, but—nothing doing! I thrust a stick under it, and bore down on the stick with all my might. Nothing doing. I mopped the sweat off my forehead and sat down on my find, trying to think what I should do next.

It was about the size of a locomotive wheel, this wretched kopek, and it was made of stone. Half a ton, it must have weighed. A crane might have lifted it, but I was no crane.

Well, I couldn't sit there forever. I jumped up and started shouting. "Help! Help!" I cried. "Help! I've found some money!"

A crowd collected. Everyone seemed to think it was a wonderful joke. "Whose kopek?" I asked.

No one answered. I should think they wouldn't. As if anyone in his senses would want to break his back on account of a kopek!

But they helped me get it up on edge, and then we sent it rolling down the hillside.

Faster and faster it rolled, wobbling dangerously at every bump in the road and frightening all passers half to death. No fun, to be run down by a whole kopek!

People here keep their money in sheds, piled up like so much firewood. Nobody guards it, and nobody ever steals it. There used to be thieves, I'm told, long, long ago; but they all died of overstrain.

That I can easily believe.

## BING-BANG, THE HUNTER

The real test of friendship is trouble. That holds true everywhere.

When I fell ill, my neighbour Bing-Bang dropped in to visit me. Bing-Bang is a hunter. It was he that taught me to hunt duckshot with the aid of a duck.

I was very glad to see him.

"Would you like to hear some stories?" Bing-Bang asked. "I can tell you all about dog powder, and pointer pigs, and carnivorous antelopes, and herbivorous wolves."

Dear, kind Bing-Bang! How well he knew that a hunter's tales are the best medicine for an ailing hunter!

"I can tell you, too," he went on, "about the way we saved all the lions and leopards from drowning."

I settled down blissfully to listen. I already felt better!

### Dog Powder

"This was a long time ago," Bing-Bang began. "When I wasn't Bing-Bang yet, but only a little boy named Bing. My Dad had a harehound, Diana, he called it—a wonderful dog. It chased an eight-legged hare, once, three days and three nights on end, and after that it fell down and

died. To keep Diana's memory fresh, Dad had a hunting jacket made out of her hide. And wasn't that a jacket! It would pull Dad straight to where the game was hiding, and shoot its buttons straight to the mark. Dad took no dogs with him to the woods in those days, yet he always came home heavy loaded."

"Mmm.... I believe I've read something of the sort somewhere," I ventured faintly.

"Perhaps," Bing-Bang returned carelessly. "Perhaps you have. But let's get on with the story. Nothing, as we all know, goes on forever. Dad's hunting jacket eventually shot away all its buttons, and ripped apart in every seam, and crumbled away into dust. Dad collected the dust, and put it in a box, and gave it to me. The hounds I was hunting with at that time were great-grandchildren of poor dead Diana, but they were lazy, disobedient curs, nothing like their great-grandma, fond of nothing so much as a good dinner and a good sleep after it. In the woods they would 'lick my spurs', as hunters put it—in other words, trail drearily at my heels. It seemed as though no force on earth could make them chase off after a hare.

"Well, and then I started mixing a bit of Diana's dust into their food before every hunting trip. And I wish you could have seen how it worked on them! They would strain at the leash with all their might, hurrying me to the woods, and the minute I loosed them, off they'd be after a hare; and they'd keep after that poor hare till it got so tired it fell in its tracks. Then they'd grab it by the ears and drag it back to me.

"Hares—they're foxy creatures, but nothing they could do could throw my hounds off the trail. I'd come home from the woods with as much game as I could carry.

"Poor old Diana! No rest for her even in the grave, with her dust being used to make her great-grandchildren work."

### Old Man Mazai and the Elephants

"I'm an old man now," Bing-Bang went on, "and I've lost my taste for hunting. It's the simplest thing in the world, after all, to go around killing bird and beast. What I really like is stories like your Russian one about Old Man Mazai. And, you know, one day I followed his example.

"There was a terrible flood, once, in our parts. Forests and steppe-land—everything under water. All our woodland beasts were in danger of drowning.

"I threw together a huge raft and hurried to the rescue. Only, don't you see, that Mazai of yours had it easy: grab a bunny by the ears, and dump it in your boat, and that's that. Whereas out here it wasn't hares, perched up in the trees and on the high spots. It was elephants and rhinos, lions and leopards. Try and catch them by the ears, or by the tail either! You'd be more likely to be caught yourself! It looked as if I'd be in more danger than them!

"So I had to turn back. I got some friends together and set them to work making more rafts. And in the meantime I ran home for bow and arrows, and to the druggist's for some sleeping powders.

"Then we set out, a regular fleet of rafts. This time things went much better. When we reached an island I'd get out an arrow, and sprinkle its tip with sleeping powder, and let it off at the nearest lion or leopard. The beast would yawn, and scratch a bit, and fall asleep. You should have heard the snoring! And then we could grab it by nape and tail and swing it onto the raft. When we had a full load we'd bring it to shore, unload, and make off for more.

"The elephants and rhinos were harder, though. My arrows glanced off their hides without so much as scratching them. And anyway, what good would it have done to put them to sleep? We couldn't have lifted them onto the rafts in any case, because, you see, an elephant weighs something like five tons. We didn't know what to do. But we hunters are resourceful folk, and I soon thought up a way. I put aside my bow and arrows and got myself a good long switch. And with that I was able to drive all the elephants and rhinos from their flooded islands into the water, and make them swim to shore. And so all the beasts were saved.

"By this time the lions and leopards were awake again, and the beasts all ran off together into the woods.

" 'Hi!' I called after them. 'Remember Old Man Mazai!' "

### Herbivorous Wolves

"I don't know about your country," Bing-Bang went on, "but in our parts grass is what the wolves like best. You can often see them grazing in forest clearings. And by night they get into the vegetable gardens. I've seen them in my own garden, more than once. They burrow under the fence and make straight for the melon beds. And in the winter they get so bold with hunger, they raid the village fields in packs and dig up whatever vegetables got left behind at harvest time. There's a saying we have about that: 'Only a fool will let the wolf into the garden.' "

"We use that saying too," I exclaimed. "But we put it this way: 'Only a fool will let the goat into the garden.' "

Bing-Bang stared.

"The goat?" he cried. "But what would a goat want in a garden? Goats are carnivores. What they want is meat."

"Not in our parts," I returned. "Our goats won't touch meat. What they want is cabbage."

"Of all the queer things!" said Bing-Bang. "You seem to live in the most topsy-turvy country! Goats that eat cabbage, and wolves that don't—it's simply incredible!"

I did not answer.

"Well, as to our goats," Bing-Bang went on, "they're confirmed beasts of prey, just like the antelopes and gazelles and all that sort. What they want is meat. The antelopes are the slyest. They manage to catch birds, even—creep up unnoticed, and down comes a hoof on the bird's head. And don't they gobble them, feathers and all. We've a saying about that, too: 'Only a fool will let an antelope into the poultry yard.' "

"Our saying is a little different," I remarked. "It goes this way: 'Only a fool will let a wolf into the sheepfold.' "

"How silly!" said Bing-Bang. "What would a wolf want in a sheepfold? Except, maybe, a quiet corner to sleep in?"

For a while, Bing-Bang said nothing more. Clearly, he found it amazing that there was a land in which all the people had short necks like mine; a land in which the men wore trousers and the women skirts, and wolves ate sheep, and goats ate cabbage.

It's a queer world, isn't it?

# A Gigantic Nest

"If you aren't tired," Bing-Bang said, "I can tell you another story, about a huge bird nest I once ran up against.

"High—no, that's not the word for it. It was lofty, towering, a regular mountain of a nest, thrown together of sand and twigs and branches and all sorts of forest refuse.

"It must have weighed a hundred and fifty tons, maybe even more.

"The nest was stuffed with birds' eggs. And the eggs lay there untended, incubating themselves. All the birds do is build the nest and lay the eggs. When the time comes the chicks hatch independently, and go running off wherever they please. Mound birds, some people call them."

Bing-Bang gave me a questioning glance before going on.

"That lake of ours—you know how blue it is. Well, then, there have been times when it was red instead of blue. And another thing: the

crocodiles come there to cry. They all get together on one of the sand bars, and cry and cry, till the lake is flooded with their crocodile tears. It's the heat that makes them cry. We humans sweat in hot weather; dogs let their tongues loll out; but crocodiles have to cry. And their tears are full of salt.

6—2371

"There's a creature in our woods so lazy—believe it or not—that it gets all grown over with moss. The moss grows on its hair, and feeds on its breath. What this creature likes best of all is sleeping. You come across one of them, and you don't even want to shoot it—just a clump of moss, up there in the treetop, nothing alive about it!

"And what do you say to our clouds?"

"What do you want me to say? They're perfectly ordinary clouds."

"Just you lick them once, and then we'll see. Our clouds are salty, that's what! The crane herder told me—he's tried it, so he ought to know. And it's not only the clouds. The snow is often salty, and so is the hoarfrost. That's the sort of thing that happens on our planet!"

### A Pointer Pig

"I still go out to the woods, but it's not what I call hunting. Where have my fine guns got to, and my keen hounds? In place of a gun I carry a wicker basket, and in place of hounds I take along a pig.

"Some hunters train dogs to help them. Some train falcons. My main helper, nowadays, is a pig. Yes, an ordinary pig—hog—curly-tailed swine. You should see it point, though—like a statue, from its silly snout to its curlicue tail.

"Dogs and falcons are used for hunting game. What I hunt, with my faithful pig, is fungi.

"I take up my basket, and whistle to my pig, and off we go. As soon as the pig smells a fungus, it stops and points. Then I come up and say, 'Dig,' and the pig begins rooting in the soil with its snout, and in another minute I have the fungus in my basket. Not just any old fungus, of course. The ones I hunt are good to eat, like mushrooms. They don't look like mushrooms, though—not at all. No stalk, no cap. And they grow underground, where you can't see them. To tell you the truth, I don't even know what they're called.

"Well, and that's how I spend my time, nowadays: basket in hand, pig on my leash, hunting I know not where and finding I know not what. Like a fairy-tale!"

## SAILOR TOPMAST'S TALES

Landlubbers—they can't even listen properly when a sailor talks of his adventures.

A horny-handed old salt will say, perhaps:

"The weather spoiled. The ship tossed and pitched and rolled. I was at the helm, peering ahead through the fog. A huge wave swept the deck, and carried me overboard. Up I flew to the wave crest, and then down its side, like sledding down a hill, into the hollow. Farewell, Mother, farewell, Father, never will you see your son again! But the next wave caught me up too, and slid me straight back to my old place on deck. And there I stood again at the helm, peering ahead through the fog—only soaking wet from head to toe."

The landlubbers laugh till they're half dead. Now, what do they find so funny?

Or, perhaps, the sailor will say:

"Or take that time in the tropics. In arm's reach of the Equator, we were, and the heat was terrific. The ship boy's skin was peeling like birch bark, and the cook had sunstroke. And there comes an iceberg, sailing our way. And what an iceberg! The height of a fifteen-storey house, and the length of it—may the sharks get me if I'm lying!—the length of it was a hundred and twenty miles if it was an inch! We had fun, I can tell you: sleigh-riding, ice-skating, skiing. And half naked too—in nothing but shorts. We were in the tropics, after all."

And again the landlubbers laugh themselves sick.

"One day," the sailor will begin again, tugging at the ring in his ear, "a fish attacked us. Came rushing straight at us, and stuck its snout right through the bottom. And before we could patch up the first hole, it made another, and another, till the whole bottom was like a sieve. Such a bottom, too—oak timbers, and steel plating."

"Oak timbers, did you say?" the landlubbers will ask.

"Yes, the timbers were oak."

"And steel plating?"

"And steel plating."

The landlubbers roar with laughter.

And the sailor turns his back on these ignorant landsmen, and tells them no more tales.

There are sailors out here too. One of them came to see me the other day. Topmast, his name was. It was a pleasant evening we had, with my toadstool lamp softly glowing, and my snail crooning to itself, and my boa curled up in its corner. Topmast's stories kept me listening breathlessly.

## Fish Catch Fish

"The most amazing things," he began, "happen to us sailors.

"It has long been common knowledge that the biggest fish is always the one that gets away. Well, and what's so strange about that? The

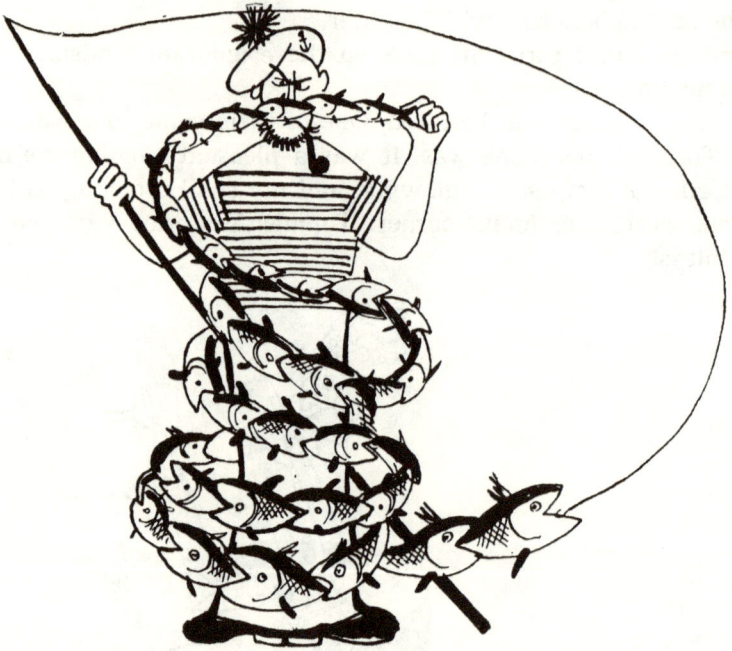

bigger the fish, the more chance it has of snapping the line and getting off. So that there's no fair ground for all those knowing smiles you see when a fisher spreads his arms to show the size of the fish he hooked but lost. There are fish in the seas bigger than any angler has ever hooked. I saw one myself, once—away out in the ocean, this was. It stood on its head at the sea bottom, and its tail stuck up nine or ten feet above the surface. There's no hook made that could hold a fish like that. Well, and who wants it? Small fish are more to my taste.

"I was out at sea, once, in my boat. I stuck my head in the water to find out whether there were any fish around. That's what I always do. I can tell by the fish voices whether there's anything around worth catching. Because, after all, who wants to cast a line for nothing?

"Well, that day I heard plenty of fish, so I threw in my line. I got a bite right off. But I didn't pull in. I just sat there, waiting. And sure enough, another fish caught on to the first one's tail. And a third caught on to the second one's tail, and then a fourth caught on, and a fifth...."

"And a sixth," I put in.

"Just so, my young friend, a sixth. And then I pulled in my line. And so it went: half a dozen fish at every cast, hanging together like a string of beads. They simply begged to be caught.

"Wouldn't that be a sight for all those summer-resort anglers, staring for hours on end at their motionless floats!

"There! You're laughing too! But you're making a big mistake, because fishers always have adventures no one else could even dream of."

## In the Belly of a Whale

"Let me tell you about one very disagreeable adventure I had, away out at sea. I mean the time I got swallowed by a whale. No one believes me when I tell them I came out of a whale's belly alive. But I did! I've been telling people this story for years, now, and not a soul but laughs at me. I've reached a point where I hardly believe it myself. But, just the same, it's true.

"Sailing along, one day, we sighted a whale. The captain ordered a boat out. I took the rudder, the men gripped their oars, and we made for the monster as fast as we could go. The whale soon noticed us. It drew a deep breath, then spouted noisily. There was no time to be lost. At my command, two harpoons shot out and stuck in the whale's flank. And then the trouble began. With a great lash of its tail, the creature upset our boat and sent us all flying into the air, like a human fountain. Coming down, I suddenly realised that I was heading straight for the whale's open jaws. I just had time to pull my knees up to my chest, to make myself as small and round as I could. The next instant I was

flying down the whale's gullet. I'd slipped through the mouth smooth as a pill, never catching on those conical teeth. Well, I thought to myself, there's that much to the good.

"The whale didn't even seem to notice it had swallowed anything. Down the slippery gullet I flew, and landed, willy-nilly, in the whale's stomach.

"Dark as night it must have been in there, I suppose you're thinking. Well, that's not your fault. It's just that you've never been in a whale's stomach.

"The stomach was brightly lit. Handsome pale-blue lights shone everywhere. By their glow, I was able to look myself over and make sure that all my limbs were sound. Well, sound limbs are a very good thing, and the place was light enough and warm enough to please anybody. But, as I soon found, I had little ground for rejoicing. There was such a stench I couldn't breathe, and my head began to spin, worse and worse, until finally I fainted. It was several weeks before I came to, and found myself in a hospital on the coast.

"I was soon well and cheerful again. But I'll be striped like a zebra all the rest of my life, because the whale had begun to digest me. However, I'd rather be striped than turned—at best—into a bit of ambergris, the product of whalish indigestion, floating to eternity on the ocean waves."


### The Size of Waves

"It's an old argument between us sailors and those stay-at-home land-lubbers: how big can the biggest wave be? There's one of them has it all figured out on paper, that there can't be a wave at sea more than twenty-six feet high. Ha, ha! Twenty-six feet, away out at sea—the height of a two-storey house—do you call that a wave? And what about a ten-storey house, you stick-on-land cowards—how would that suit you? Scary, eh? A regular mountain of a wave, with a snow-white crest, rolling along at the speed of a jet plane. I met up with one wave that circled the planet three times around.

"Well, and what would you say to a wave the height of a fifteen-

storey house? And a hundred and twenty-five miles long? Not to your taste, eh? You know only too well that a wave like that, if it swept over your city, wouldn't leave a one of you pen-pushers alive. A wave like that can lift a great ship out of the water and cast it ashore like an empty sea shell. It can make ships fly like planes—I've flown that way myself. That's the sea for you—as sailors see it, not landlubbers, building sand castles on the beach."

My sailor friend gulped down his tea and made for the door, feeling his way in the semidarkness. Before leaving, he kicked my poor boa and spat at my singing snail.

"Drones! Moles! Earthworms!" I could hear him grumbling as he went down the street. "What can you know about the sea?"

# THE DIVER'S TALES

Attracted by the rumour that I never questioned what people told me, Bubble-Bub, the local diver, also came to see me.

Pausing at the threshold, he asked suspiciously:

"Can you believe in a shark swallowing a padlock, half a sack of potatoes, and a pair of tarpaulin trousers?"

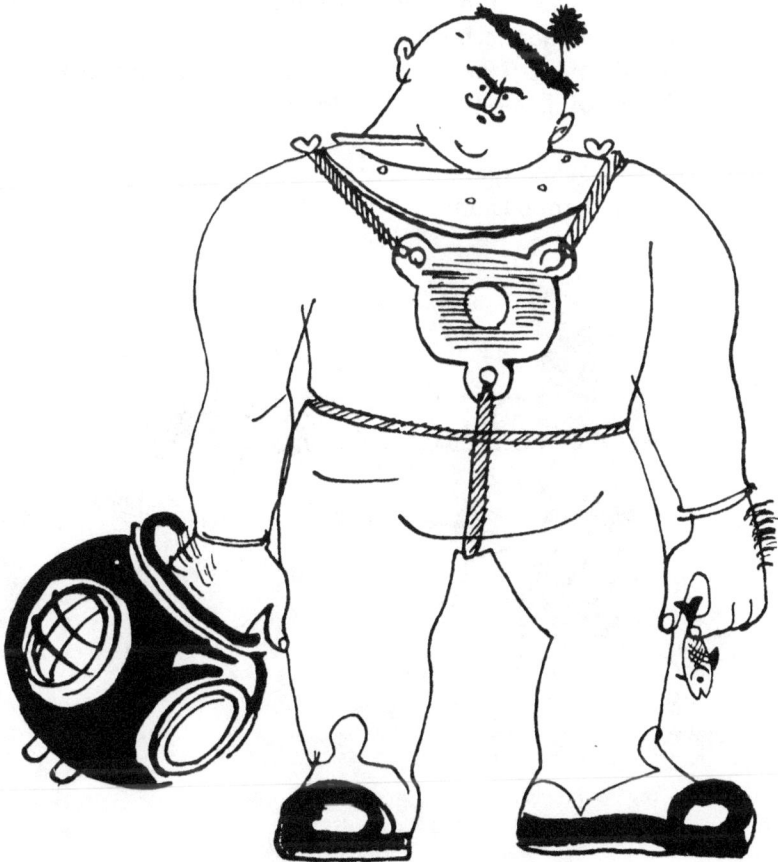

"I can," I responded obligingly.

"Ah! Then I'll come in. Drive away your boa and light up your fish. I've got some tales to tell you."

Bubble-Bub rubbed his cheeks with both hands, then laid his huge fists on the table and inquired fiercely:

"What colour is your blood?"

"Red," I squeaked.

"Mine is green," the diver thundered.

### Green Blood

"Everyone tries to make me believe that human blood is red, and animal and bird blood too, and even the blood of fish. But they can't fool me! I don't know about birds and animals—a diver has nothing much to do with them, so I can't argue. But as far as my own blood goes, and the blood of fish—there I stand firm, because I 've seen it with my own eyes.

"A hammer fish attacked me, one day. Yes, that's what I said, a hammer fish. It's got a hammer instead of a head. And a big one, too.

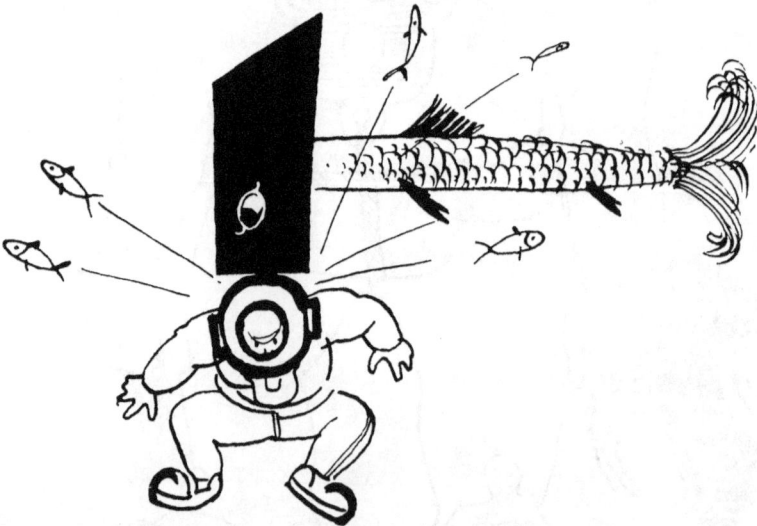

"Well, it banged me on the back with its hammer, and I dropped face down in the slime.

"I began wriggling and twisting, trying to pull myself out of the mud —when down came the hammer again, on my fingers this time. I got so angry, I struck back with my knife. And I saw the blood run. From my fingers and from the fish's side. And what colour do you think it was? It was green. Green. Green.

"And there was nothing out of the ordinary about it, I want you to remember. Green is simply the normal colour for blood. Just as the normal colour of leaves and grasses is orange. Well, and what's bothering you now? It's the truth I'm telling you. Come, now, is it orange, or isn't it?"

"Yes, yes," I hastened to answer. "The colour of leaves is orange, and the colour of blood is green."

"That's better," the diver responded. He leaned back in his chair, his whole body convulsed by soundless laughter.


### Red Tide

"What *is* red at times," he said, "is the tide."

"The tide is green," I protested.

"It's red," the diver declared. And he shifted his fists to the edge of the table. "It's red. Have you got that straight?"

"Oh, yes."

"What colour is the tide?"

"Red."

"And what colour are leaves?"

"Orange."

"And blood?"

"Green."

"That's better. Well, then, when the red tide comes rolling in, the fish begin to die. The waves come rolling, and the fish all die."

"The fish all die," I repeated after him.

"And the crabs die too," he continued.

"And the crabs too."

"And the mollusks."

"And the mollusks."

"And the people on shore begin to cough and cry."

"And sneeze," I ventured.

"You're quite right," the diver returned, so pleased that he raised a fist and brought it smashing down on the table. The table groaned and almost tumbled over.

"Do you believe me now?" he demanded, looking me straight in the eye.

"Of course, of course," I twittered weakly.

### Dolphins Play Ball

"Have you ever seen dolphins play basketball?" the diver asked.

"I have," I answered.

"Oh, no you haven't," he retorted venomously.

"Very well. I haven't," I agreed.

"Well, then, you just listen to me. Dolphins play basketball no worse than humans. In the water, of course. They pass the ball, and catch the ball, and throw it up into the basket. With their snouts. Get it in every time."

He looked at me searchingly, but I held my tongue.

"They've got their rooters, too," he went on. "The seals. While the dolphins are playing, the seals sit watching on the bank, roaring and clapping their flippers, in a fever of excitement."

I held my tongue.

"And after the game you can take a ride on the captain of the team."

I held my tongue.

"And you can send it down to fetch you pearl shells from the sea bottom."

I held my tongue.

"There!" he breathed, with a sigh of relief. "And at first you wouldn't believe me!"

## At the Bottom of the Sea

"I spent a whole week, once, at the bottom of the sea, and you can't imagine all the interesting sights I saw."

"What kept you there so long?"

"I stumbled on a shell, and it caught my foot and wouldn't let it go. A huge shell, that was. Must have weighed half a ton."

"Well, and what did you eat down there, all that time?"

"What would you expect me to eat at the bottom of the sea? Sea kale, of course, and sea cucumbers."

"And what did you drink?"

"That's no problem at sea. There's no end of springs at the sea bottom, and their water is cool and fresh."

"Well and good. And what did you see that was so interesting?"

"Ha! What didn't I see? I saw the sea devils dance. Big black devils, with horns and wings. They take a good run, and up they leap out of the water, ten feet into the air. And then down they come flat on their bellies, smashing the waves out of shape. Wide across as a bus, and weigh a ton or more. Sea food is nourishing!

"There was a nice jellyfish, too. About the height of a ten-storey house. Pretty to look at, giving off a greenish glow.

"And then there was the living grass, a whole field of it. Swaying like a field of rye in the wind. But the minute I stirred it disappeared, hiding away in its burrows.

"I saw a lady octopus brooding its eggs in a basket made of its own tentacles.

"And a lady perch and its perchlets out for a stroll along the sea floor, just like a hen and its chicks in the barnyard. Only a hen hides its chicks under its wings when danger threatens, whereas a perch takes its young into its mouth and makes off with them as fast as it can go.

"I saw an electric fish, with a set of batteries on its side.

"And a cuttlefish with a jet engine that made it fly like an arrow from the bow."

"Did you see any fish with steam engines?" I asked.

"No, I didn't notice any."

I heaved a sigh of relief.

The diver got up, wagged a warning finger before my nose, and left.

I heaved another sigh of relief.


## MY FRIEND MAGMA, THE GEOLOGIST

Day had hardly broken when I was wakened by a terrific pounding at the door.

I was frightened for a moment, thinking it might be the diver back again.

But it turned out to be Magma, the geologist, banging at the door with his prospecting hammer.

Unlike my earlier visitors, he was a short, slight little man, with ears like cabbage leaves and a nose like a pear.

Unlike the others, too, he had come not to tell me tales, but to show me about. That was good news. You can learn more about a thing by seeing it, if only once, than by hearing about it any number of times.


### A Musical Mountain

We reached a mountain made of sand. And when we started up its side the mountain began to sing, as if we were treading not sand, but the keyboard of a giant organ. It made loud sounds and soft, blaring and gentle; you could distinguish fiddles, flutes, and drums. A pleasant experience, but rather creepy!

Magma only smiled at my amazement, and flapped his cabbage-leaf ears.

Suddenly he took a run, squatted on his heels, and went sliding down the far side of the mountain. What a thundering broke out, what an angry beating of drums! Magma waved a beckoning hand, and I too took a run and went sliding down the mountain to the accompaniment of thunder and beating drums.

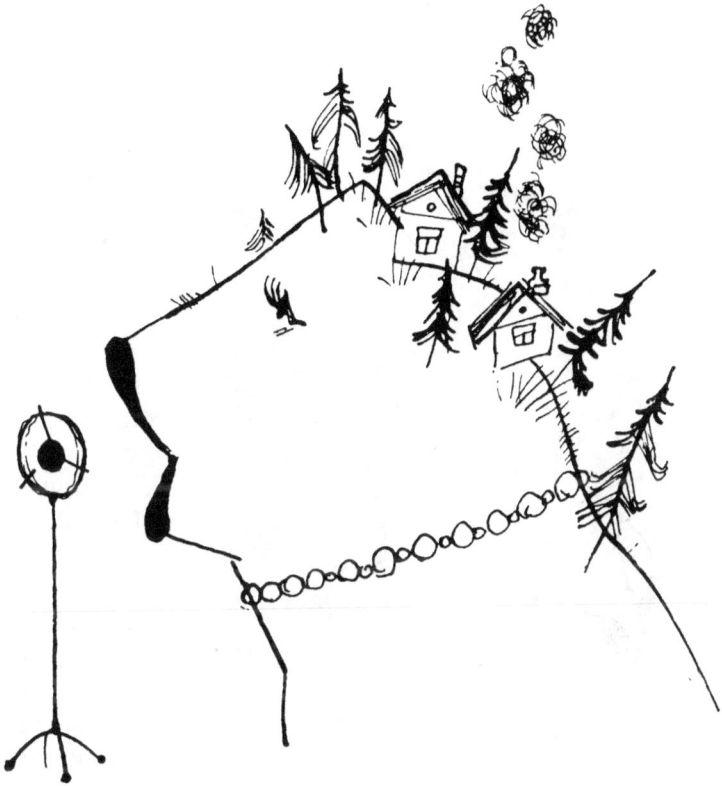

My companion was highly pleased. And so was I.

The mountain stood before us, playing and singing. And we stood staring at it, with never a word to say.

### Flowers That Talk

Down in the valley, Magma suddenly forgot all about me. The valley was full of flowers, and he seemed in a great hurry to pick some.

He snatched the blossoms hastily, but then gave each of them a thorough look-over and carefully noted down his observations. His lips kept twitching soundlessly, as though he were having a conversation with the flowers—asking them questions and considering their replies.

Was he really a geologist, I wondered, or was he, perhaps, a botanist? Or, perhaps, a poet?

"What are you whispering about?" I asked him.

"I've found a treasure," he replied. "There's incalculable riches in this valley, deep underground."

"How do you know?" I asked.

"The flowers told me," he replied. "The flowers."

Stranger and stranger, I reflected. Flowers that set forests afire, flowers that grow underground, and now, to top it all, flowers that talk!

"They're clever, our flowers," Magma cried. "They know every treasure that lies hidden underground. You need only learn their language, and they'll tell you everything you want to know."

Magma seemed happy as a king, admiring his armful of flowers, drinking in their fragrance, plaiting them into a wreath. He thurst one of the blossoms into my buttonhole.

I dried it, when I got home, and shall always treasure it.

When we started digging at the spot where this blossom had grown, our spades soon struck something hard. It turned out to be a great lump of pure gold.

So that, as you see, some of the flowers that grow on this Topsy-Turvy Planet can be very useful.

Thanks to my friends, I'm well and cheerful again. They know how to fight the dumps. First they cheered me up, then they amused me, then they provoked me a bit, and finally they lured me out of doors. And I've lost all desire to lie around in bed.

## AN ETERNAL STEW

My illness left me thin as a shadow—thinner, even.

To fatten me up a bit, my fisher friends brought me a pailful of live fish. The fish were so lively and so pretty, I hadn't the heart to cook them. So I searched out a big jar, filled it full of clear, cool spring water, and dumped the fish into it so they wouldn't die.

But they seemed determined to die. They dropped to the bottom of the jar, every one of them, and lay there like so many stones.

So that I had no choice about it. The only thing to do with them, clearly, was to stew and eat them.

I built up a fire, hung a pot of water over it, threw in the fish, and clamped down the lid.

Soon the water boiled.

I lifted the lid to stir my stew. But there wasn't any stew to stir. All my dead fish had come alive again, and were darting about in the boiling water as merry as can be. When I threw in some meal to thicken the stew, they were only too pleased.

In two ticks, they had gobbled down all the meal. No stew for me!

And now there's always a good fire burning in my room, with a steaming pot hung over it, and my pretty fish in the pot.

Day after day I cook this stew, but I'm afraid it will never be done, because the minute I throw in some meal the fish eat it all up.

The fish get fatter and fatter, but I get thinner and thinner. My collar has got so loose, I can look down through it and see my shoes.

## A BIRD THAT EATS NAILS

Birds that eat grain are termed granivorous. Birds that eat insects are termed insectivorous. What term, then, is a person to apply to a bird that eats nails?

That's what my friends brought me, the other day: a bird that eats nails.

"Nails? Not really?" I demanded.

"Yes," they said, "nails. And plenty else besides."

They brought me the bird as a great treat, to cook for my dinner. They'd fattened it specially for me, they said.

I plucked it, and singed it, and laid it open. And when I got to the stomach, I found it full of nails.

Copper nails, steel nails, iron nails. And not only nails. Sand, tow, rags, bits of iron, copper coins, hinges, keys, little balls of lead, buttons, bells, pebbles, cigarette butts, splintered wood, bits of glass, thread, pencils, tacks, and an indiarubber eraser.

The most surprising thing about it, though, was not so much the bird's strange choice of diet as the fact that, living on such food, it

seemed very well-fed. I weighed it, just to see, and the scale said two hundred pounds—a good weight for three sheep!

Even piscivorous birds never grow to such size—and fish, after all, is so nutritious!

## A GREAT FEAST

My friends gave a great feast today to celebrate the harvest home. I was invited, with the warning that there would be no less than a hundred different dishes, and that I would be expected to sample every one of them. An alarming prospect, but how could I refuse? My friends might have been hurt.

The best seat at table had been reserved for me. I sat down, rubbing my hands together in anticipation and breathing deep of the delicious fragrance of cooking, roasting, frying. I took up my knife and fork, opened my mouth, and—sat there staring, unable to believe my eyes.

A big crane was lowering to the table a frying pan that held fifty thousand portions of fried fish, hissing in oil.

Yes, that was a frying pan! Ten couples could have danced on it, and not been crowded.

The fifty thousand guests took a portion each, and the empty pan was removed.

The fish course was followed by a succession of local delicacies. First came dried frogs, a dish of snakes, and cuttlefish eggs, and after those sea slugs and bamboo salad.

I waited patiently, wondering—what next?

Next were birds' nests, and fried ants, and locusts. Also, to go with the tea, bee milk and young bee larvae.

Furtively, I looked up and down the table. All the guests were talking and laughing, obviously enjoying their food. Many asked for second helpings.

Bears' blood was offered, and nasturtium salad; locust cakes, and rusks made of caterpillars, and pies with a filling of May bug larvae.

I shut my eyes.

New dishes were brought, but I did not see them. I laid down my knife and fork, put away my crumpled napkin, and wandered weakly homeward. I had had enough.

At home, I nibbled happily at a dry bread crust. In the village, the guests feasted on without me.

## MONUMENT TO A BUG

There are no end of monuments in these parts, big and small. It's the custom here, you see, to put a monument up to anyone who has furthered the common good.

I was invited, one day, to attend the unveiling of a monument to a bug.

It came of no high family, this bug. Looked like some common sort of fly, or maybe aphis. Yet—you'd never believe it!—this insignificant bug was the conqueror of the rabid hedges.

The thing began long years ago.

To keep wild animals from spoiling their crops, people planted a prickly hedge around their fields.

At first all went well. The prickly hedges took firm root, and soon

put an end to the disastrous inroads of wild boar, buffalo, and monkeys.

But suddenly the hedge ran wild.

It attacked the fields, and killed the crops, and fenced all the land up and down and across, and you couldn't get anywhere from anywhere else, because all the roads were blocked.

What had started it, who can tell? Perhaps the bite of a mad dog? Baron Munchausen tells such a tale, if you remember: a fur cloak, bitten by a mad dog, went mad itself and became so dangerous it had to be shot. I never really believed that story. But, after all, if a hedge can go mad, why can't a cloak?

Well, the people began to fight the hedge.

They set it afire. They chopped it down. They tore it up by the roots. They battled it day and night.

But all in vain. The hedge continued its advance across the country, fencing what it pleased and where it pleased. It barred the people off from all the world.

And then, just as hope had begun to die, this brave bug came to the rescue. It rallied its friends to the combat, and in the course of one summer they devoured the mad hedge everywhere, down to its very last twig.

The people were overjoyed, of course. Who wouldn't be? It's no fun at all, living all your life behind a prickly fence that cuts you off from the rest of the world.

And so they decided to set up a monument to the bug. A stone monument, with the inscription, "To the bugs, with deepest gratitude, for freeing our fields of the mad hedges."

So you see what a tiny bug can do.

To my mind, the monument was well deserved.


### THE GOLDEN FISH

Remember the tale about the golden fish? The one the old fisherman brought up in his net, and threw back into the sea again when it begged him in human tongue to let it go, and promised him rich ransom?

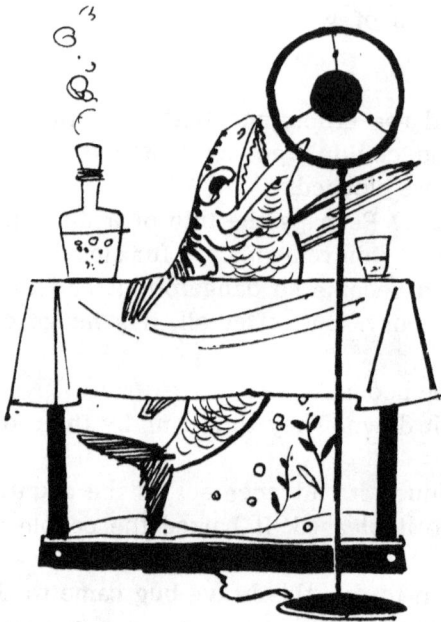

The fisherman threw the golden fish back into the sea, and it kept its promise by giving him a fine new house, and a new wooden trough to boot.

Well, that's just a tale. But the people of this Topsy-Turvy Planet have caught another fish, a real one, well worthy to be called queen of the seas.

No one remembers, now, who caught the fish, or when, or whether it really promised to be of service. Simply, as far back as memory can go, it has always been man's true helper. It doesn't build him houses, no, nor present him with wooden troughs. It does better than that: it saves countless lives.

Life is not too tranquil, in this land where mountains are able to meet. Every now and again something begins to rumble and stir underground, and everything aboveground—trees, houses, fences, lampposts, roads, and even iron rails—begins to shake and shiver with fear. Yes, and often enough things not only shake, but fall.

That is why the people build their houses of paper. It's less dangerous, after all, to be buried under the remains of a paper house than under those of a log one. Some people, too, build their houses on springs. When the earth shakes, such houses hop and skip like so many grasshoppers, but they are not destroyed.

An earthquake cannot be prevented. It cannot be stopped or restrained. And no one ever knows when it is going to strike. But this little white fish knows. The little white fish knows everything. There in its crystal palace, it stands watch. When all is well, it swims tranquilly about from corner to corner. But when danger threatens, when the

earth is soon to quake, the little fish begins a frantic darting to and fro, warning the people to flee—flee—flee.

Just a little white fish, but for this service to man everyone calls it a fish of gold.

## CLAP THE WHALE ON ITS BACK

It snowed this morning and part of the snow was black, and part red. I must hurry home before winter comes to stay.

All my new friends gathered today to say good-bye. Sailor Topmast was there, and Magma the geologist, and diver Bubble-Bub, and Bing-Bang the hunter.

We didn't talk, at first—just sat looking at one another and wondering whether we'd ever meet again, this world of ours being so very large and so replete with unsolved mysteries.

It was the diver who finally broke the silence.

"There's a saying in your country," he began, "about the sea. That anyone who's so much as glimpsed the sea will be sure to come back to it. Well, and in our country we say too that anyone who's been here once, and glimpsed our topsy-turvy world, will be sure to come again."

"There's another saying, too," Magma added. " 'If you want to believe in wonders,' it goes, 'clap a whale on its back.' "

"That's right," everybody cried. "Let's go and do just that!"

"Let's," I responded. "Why not?"

Yes, even in parting, my Topsy-Turvy Planet proved its worth. Try and clap a whale on its back anywhere else! Nothing doing! But here—any time you please!

We took along a pick and broke a hole in the ice, a good way out to sea. We had not long to wait. Soon the water in the hole began to seethe, and a whale put out its head to breathe. Each of us in turn clapped the creature on its broad, wet shoulder. And at once we felt that we could believe in any wonder.

The whale looked us up and down and spouted prodigiously.

Then it drew a deep breath and disappeared under the ice. The water remained troubled long after the whale was gone.

It's true. Once you've clapped a whale on its back, you'll never forget it. You'll never again doubt the wonders of the Topsy-Turvy Planet, and you'll be sure, some day, to go again to that fascinating land where the impossible becomes possible and the ordinary extraordinary; this land where fiction becomes truth, and truth resembles fiction.

And if there is still anyone who won't believe that land exists, I earnestly advise him to lose no time in clapping a whale on its wet back. It's so very simple!

## HOME AGAIN

Here I am, home again.

Only yesterday I walked that amazing soil, admired those amazing blossoms, climbed those amazing mountains, threaded those amazing forests. Only yesterday I breathed the air of that amazing planet, and drank of its water. And it was no dream or fancy. My feet stood firmly on the ground. Yet as soon as I got home all I had seen and experienced was enveloped in a bluish haze that transformed it once more into a distant, distant dream. Had I really been there, I began to wonder, or had I only imagined it?

Be that as it may, however, I've fulfilled my promise. I've set down the tale of my amazing adventures, and I've set it down truthfully, just as it really happened.

## THE TOPSY-TURVY PLANET

Shaking his head, the editor laid down the manuscript and leaned back in his chair.

"Ummm," he said drily. "An amazing planet!"

"Topsy-turvy," Paramon responded.

"Well, and how did you get back home?"

"That was easy. I just stepped across the threshold and shut the door behind me."

"How nice!" the editor said, frowning. "Was that on April first, by any chance?"

"That's right. On April Fool's Day."

"Jokes aside," the editor insisted. "By what name do astronomers call this Topsy-Turvy Planet?"

"By the same name everyone calls it."

A breeze rustled the papers on the editor's desk.

"Look at the sky," Paramon suggested. "See all the planets twinkling at us out of the black—every one of them a mysterious world of its own.

"On one planet there is no morning and no evening, only day and night. On another, eternal night reigns on one side, and eternal day on the other.

"So many different worlds, distant and strange.

"But there is one planet far stranger than all the rest.

"When it is summer on the upper half of this planet, it is winter on the lower half. When it is morning on one side, it is evening on the other.

"At top and bottom, it is capped with white. On the one cap, wherever you look is South. On the other, wherever you look is North. There is a great ocean on this planet, and in this ocean East meets West.

"It is simply stuffed with wonders, this Topsy-Turvy Planet.

"It is inhabited by intelligent beings, who call themselves humans. And they call their planet—Earth."

"What?" the editor cried. "Are you trying to tell me that all these adventures you've described took place here, on our Earth?"

"Exactly."

"Varicoloured suns, and dry rains, and long-necked people?"

"Yes, and coins that weigh half a ton, and underground flowers."

"And bird milk, and that eternal stew?"

"Yes, and nail-eating birds, and all the rest."

"Are you trying to make fun of me, or what?" the editor demanded

furiously. "Your stories are pure plagiary on Baron Munchausen! Munchausen strung ducks on a string with the aid of a bit of bacon, and you talk of garlands of fish caught on one hook. Munchausen talks of a huge kingfisher's nest, and you talk of a nest that weighs two hundred tons. Munchausen gets into a fish's belly, and your sailor friend gets into the stomach of a whale. And that dog powder of yours is Munchausen's waistcoat turned inside out. What are you trying to prove—that Munchausen was the most truthful man that ever lived? Your stories are impossible, every one of them. They're fantastic. They couldn't have happened."

"They could," Paramon said quietly.

"Prove it!"

"Here's the proof."

And Paramon handed the editor an ordinary grey copybook. The editor leafed it through carelessly at first, but was soon entirely absorbed by what he found in it.

*"The 'sad' thing about science is, its persistent effort to dispel the charm of mystery that still cloaks so many of Nature's secrets, great or small."*

# THE GREY COPYBOOK

*"But, as we so often observe, real life is far more fascinating, more extraordinary, than anything our imagination is capable of inventing."*

**HOLD ON!**
**DON'T TURN THIS PAGE!**

Look back over what you have just read, and think it over carefully. What seems true to you, and what false? What surprises you, and what arouses unbelief? Are such things possible on this Earth of ours, or are they not?

When you feel clear on these things, turn the page.

In this grey copybook you will find the answers to all your doubts and questions, collected by me from the pages of various magazines, bulletins, and books of science.

## RIDING SHARKBACK

Is it possible, is it at all conceivable, for a man to ride a shark?

Hans Hass, the world-famed diver, describes an encounter with a huge whale shark in the Red Sea.

The nearer it got, he confesses, the harder it became to conquer fear.

The shark's jaws were slightly parted. It had lips. For all its enormous size,

A gigantic whale shark, photographed under water by Hans Hass

∇

the creature had a good-natured, harmless look. What Hass was after was to photograph its open mouth and the dozen or so of pilot fishes that played about it, swimming fearlessly into the dark opening and out of it again. That done, the two adventurers (Hass was accompanied by a friend) clambered up onto the shark's back. Holding on to the dorsal fin, tough as tanned leather, they rode sharkback for a while. Hass had had all sorts of experiences in his fourteen years of underwater adventuring, but there had been nothing to compare with this incredible exploit. There is an old Hawaiian legend of two shipwrecked sailors who clung to the dorsal fin of a great shark, one night, and were brought safe and sound to one of the islands. After this ride, Hass readily believed the truth of that old tale.

There are no whale sharks in Soviet waters. Our largest shark is the polar one—a rapacious and dangerous creature, twenty-five feet long, found in the Barents Sea.

## CAT KINGDOM

In the Indian Ocean there is an uninhabited coral island which is pitted with countless burrows, the homes of thousands of ordinary household cats run altogether wild. By night, at the ebb tide, the cats come out of their burrows to hunt fish in the shallows.

No one knows how the cats got there. It is thought that their forebears may have reached the island with bits of wreckage from some storm-broken ship.

## RAIN

All sorts of strange rains visit this earth of ours.

There is a town in Britain where, one day, live herring came raining down on the heads of the townsfolk.

There have been rains of caterpillars, of worms, of frogs. In the Gorky Region, in 1940, it rained sand and ancient copper coins. Rain is sometimes coloured. It may be red as blood, or white as milk.

In all these cases, it is the wind that is to blame. Storm winds, sweeping over seas, forests, mountains, carry away with them now a school of herring, now an accumulation of frogs or caterpillars, only to drop them in the end, often very far away, to the amazement of all who see.

Sometimes a wind will raise worms together with the top layers of the soil; sometimes it will discover and carry off long-buried treasures.

Red rains are caused by ochre dust, or sometimes by microscopic red algae, raised by the wind. Milk-white rains owe their colouring to chalk dust.

Sometimes a rain will be dry. This generally happens over desert country, where the air is very hot. Yes, even over deserts clouds sometimes assemble, and rain begins to fall. People see the rain coming down, but they never feel it. The raindrops evaporate long before they can reach the ground. In the Soviet Union, such dry rains occur in Turkmenia and in Uzbekistan.

There are other tricks, too, that rain is liable to play—even the most ordinary, wet and colourless, of rains. There is a town in the United States—Winesburg, Ohio—in which for ninety years (1870 to 1959) it has always rained on the twenty-ninth of July. The district being inclined to drought, this rainy day has become a welcome holiday to the townspeople. Only nine times, in all these ninety years, have they been disappointed.

## THE FIRST DAY

There is only one place in the world where you can find trees with square trunks. This is in Panama, a few miles to the north of the Panama Canal. When such a tree is felled its age is counted not by rings, but by squares.

India is the home of an amazing tree called the banyan. There is one such tree known to be three thousand years old. It has three thousand thick trunks, and three thousand thin ones. From a distance, you take it for a forest in itself. Over seven thousand people can find shelter in its shade.

⊲ A garage accommodating several cars could be built in this hole in the trunk of the "Forest Mother" bread fruit tree (Madagascar)

In the Soviet Union, too, there are trees famed for their size. A plane tree growing in Azerbaijan has a trunk thirty-six feet around, and a hollow in its trunk which can hold twenty people and was at one time used as a tearoom, with two tables and ten chairs.

There is an oak in the Belovezhsk forests that is over eight hundred years old. To prolong its life still further, it is planned to give it an artificial supplementary root, made of concrete, twenty-six feet long.

A dozen men, standing at arms' ⊳ length, can barely circle the trunk of this huge sequoia, named for General Sherman (U.S.A.)

122

## VARICOLOURED SUNS

Generally speaking, the sun is red at its rising and setting, and yellow all day. But people have seen it coloured sky-blue, and darker blue, and even green. In September 1950 the sun over Germany, France, Switzerland, and Denmark was sky-blue, due to huge forest and prairie fires in Canada that filled the air with smoke and ashes. A bright blue sunset has been observed by sailors in the Strait of Gibraltar.

After the tremendous eruption of Krakatao volcano in 1883, the sun shone blue.

And after the eruption of Tambora volcano, in the Indian Ocean, in 1815, the sun turned green.

Multiple suns, too, have often been observed. During severe frosts people often see three suns in the sky—the true sun and two false ones. "Sun with ears", or "sun in mittens", our northerners call this phenomenon. It is caused by refraction of the sun's rays in passing through ice crystals floating in the air.

On April 9, 1868, eight suns were seen over the Ural Mountains.


## A GREAT DAY

There is a tribe in Burma known as the Padaungs, or Long-Necks. The women of this tribe wear on their necks a sort of frame or support of thick brass coils. The first of these coils is put on a little girl's neck when she reaches the age of five, and the fourth and last when she reaches the age of eleven. By this time the child's neck is already seven or eight inches long. When she reaches maturity, it will be twelve to sixteen inches long. The greater the length of a woman's neck, the richer and the more beautiful she is considered to be.

Brass, among the Padaungs, is considered a precious metal. Neither by day nor by night do the women remove their ornaments. Nor could they remove them if they wished; for their neck muscles are so weakened that they cannot support the weight of the head without the assistance of the spirals.

A woman of the Padaung tribe ▷

Brass ornaments are worn not only on the neck, but on the arms and legs, and even on the belly. Their total weight may be as much as twenty-two pounds.

A large spider found on certain of the tropical islands is known for the size and strength of its web. One strand of its silk, hardly four thousandths of an inch in diameter, sustains a weight of almost three ounces and can be stretched twenty-five per cent of its original length.

The islanders have learned to make this spider useful. A bamboo ring five feet across, placed in the spot where a spider has begun to spin, will soon be webbed over, making a landing net that can hold a fish weighing over three pounds. Such nets are used also for catching birds, butterflies, and bats.

In the Solomon Islands, fishermen fasten this spider's webs to wooden hoops, bait them with ants, and send them floating down the rivers. Fish attracted by the ants get entangled in the web.

Many islanders use spider silk as thread.

In China, a beautiful and durable cloth used to be made of spider silk. In Europe, too, spider silk used to be made into handsome and durable clothing. It was a laborious and lengthy process, however, nor was it a simple thing to keep thousands of greedy spiders properly fed; and the cloth and clothing made of this silk were very costly.

Artists have been known to paint on cobweb, in water colour or in India ink. After a soaking in diluted milk, the web becomes sufficiently durable for use as canvas. Cobweb paintings are generally small, no larger than an ordinary postcard. The brushes used for them are made of the feathers of the snipe.

The first artist to paint on cobweb was Elias Prünner, of the South Tyrol. In our day, cobweb paintings have been exhibited in Vienna by the Austrian painter Justinus Sodan.

## CITY SCENES

A portrait painted on cobweb (South Tyrol, Austria)

In some parts of Japan, where earthquakes are frequent, many people live in houses made of heavy paper. In the Soviet Union, there is a house in the city of Ashkhabad which stands on steel springs. In minor earthquakes such houses do not suffer, and their inhabitants hardly notice the shocks.

The Scottish national costume for men consists of a short jacket and a short tartan skirt, known as a kilt. And in the East women have worn trousers from ancient times. In our day many women in the West, too, have adopted trousers.

Aquarium earrings are always in fashion in some parts of the Americas. Made of crystal, and no larger in size than ordinary earrings, these aquariums are none the less genuine, with water inside them, and live fish in the water. These miniature fishlets, about the size of ants, are called pandacha.

All donkeys on the French island of Ré, in the Bay of Biscay, wear trousers, either striped or polka-dotted. Ré was at one time very swampy, and donkey trousers were invented to protect the animals against the mosquitoes that bred in the swamps. The swamps have since been drained, but the custom persists.

In Peking, and also in a number of other Chinese cities, you may notice people in the streets with yokes on their shoulders, from which hang clusters of tiny cages. Inside the cages you will see, not song birds, but singing insects—cicadas. The sounds these insects produce are quite pleasant, and they are readily bought. They are fed on water-melon pulp.

Dentures, in Canada, are made not only for humans, but also for cows. Good teeth are essential to good health, and a cow with a healthy set of teeth yields more milk. One veterinary dentist is said to have had ten thousand cows under observation.

Roses and mignonette are mortal foes. If they are put together in a vase, a battle to the death begins between them. The mignonette weakens rapidly, and its blossoms soon droop and die. But, dying, it emits a deadly poison which soon kills the rose as well.

Roses and carnations, set too close together, both lose their fragrance. Lily of the valley will kill any flower put into the same vase with it. Narcissus is a deadly neighbour to the innocent forget-me-not.

Our height varies not only with the years of our life, but in the course of every day.

In China and in many other of the countries of East Asia women wear trousers

▽

It is greatest, science has established, when we get up in the morning, after the night's rest. Between morning and evening it generally shrinks about three-quarters of an inch, sometimes even more. If we have done much walking during the day, our height may shrink as much as two and three-quarters inches. This is due to compression of the cartilage in our spines.

## A PAGE FROM MY DIARY

In 1955 a mountain in Germany called Bärenkopf, or Bear's Head, suddenly began to move, advancing on the nearby village of Gunzesried at the rate of three and a quarter feet a day. It was several weeks before this movement stopped. All the roads in the vicinity were ruined, and new hills and fissures appeared in the village fields and pastures.

Scientists are still seeking an explanation of this rare phenomenon.

Our earth, generally speaking, is not at all so firm and changeless as we are inclined to think it.

Between 1880 and 1951 the German town of Lüneburg sank six and a half feet into the earth. Many of its houses became uninhabitable.

And then there are the tides, which affect not only the seas, but the land as well. Tides are caused by the attraction of the moon. In the vicinity of Moscow, for example, at high tide, the surface rises about twelve inches.

Besides tidal changes, there are other processes that lift the earth's crust in some places and depress it in others. It has been established that in the vicinity of Moscow the earth's crust sinks eight hundredths of an inch yearly, while in the vicinity of Lvov it rises sixteen hundredths of an inch.

*128*

# A WHITE BLACK RAVEN

Sportsmen, one day, brought down a strange bird, very like a raven, but entirely white. It was a raven, all right, and the only unusual thing about it was its white colouring, caused by an insufficiency of pigment. This condition,

A white tiger
▽

known as albinism, occurs among the most varied types of creatures, even those which are normally of the darkest colouring. There are albino sparrows, jackdaws, rooks, grouse, capercaillie, eagles; wolves, tigers, elephants, deer, moles, martens. Two white grass snakes, with pink eyes, were once caught in the Voronezh Region. White frogs, too, have been displayed in zoos. These frogs and snakes were so transparent that many of their internal organs were clearly visible through the skin.

A new type of tree frog was discovered in Mexico in the spring of 1954. The skin of its belly was so transparent that everything inside it could be clearly seen.

### UNDERGROUND FLOWERS

In Australia, one day, a farmer, digging in his fields, discovered flowers blooming at a depth of twelve inches underground. From a horizontal rhizome, or rootstock, rose thick white stems, carrying large buds that resembled orchids.

This underground "orchid" grows, blossoms, and yields seed in complete darkness. It is pollinated, perhaps, by the earthworm.

Its blossoms have an amazing way of changing colour. At one moment pale pink, they may at the next be violet.

They were unknown to science until 1928.

### SINGING SNAILS

If fish have voices, why shouldn't snails?

There is a snail in Burgundy that sleeps through the winter, and again through the summer droughts, but when the warm rains fall begins to sing—at any rate, to emit sounds that resemble singing.

### THE SPECKLED HEN

A hen at the Voronezh experimental station once laid an egg. Not an ordinary egg. A double one. The egg weighed five and a third ounces. Inside it were a white and yolk, as usual, and also a second egg, weighing an ounce and three quarters.

A triple egg, too, has been recorded. This egg weighed nine and one third ounces. It had no shell. Inside it were two normal eggs.

Pigeons have also been known to lay double eggs.

## SCARE-FEATHERS

It has long been known that certain birds, when frightened, tend to lose their feathers. An attempt to catch them, or even to approach them suddenly, especially when they are asleep, makes them shed their tail feathers completely, and often part of the wing feathers as well.

Onagadori cocks
▽

After such a loss new feathers generally grow in sooner than after an ordinary moulting.

Among the birds that lose their feathers when frightened are pheasants, pigeons, turkeys, thrushes, titmice, canaries, partridge, and many others. But there is a Japanese cock called onagadori that never loses its tail feathers. This breed was developed artificially over a century and a half ago. The tail feathers of the onagadori cock grow all its life, and by the time the cock is four years old its tail is generally ten feet long. One such cock is known to have grown a twenty-three -foot tail, so that when it perched on the roof of a two-storey house its tail reached the ground. These fowl are under official protection in Japan.

## POACHING FOR FROGS

The goliath frog, the largest in the world, grows to a length of twelve and a half inches. The North American bullfrog grows to be seven or eight inches long, and weighs as much as a pound and a quarter. The bullfrog is edible, its "hams" being particularly valued.

Frog hunters in the United States take something like a hundred million of these frogs annually—50,000 tons.

There are various ways of hunting frogs. They may be netted, or hooked, or shot. The frog season is strictly limited by law.

The bullfrog lives on mollusks and insects. At times it captures small fish, or the young of aquatic birds. Its spring song resembles the bellowing of a herd of bulls. It can be heard two miles off.

The largest frog known in the Soviet Union is the lake frog, which grows to a length of six and a half inches. This frog eats insects and worms. Sportsmen once saw a lake frog catch a small bird.

## MY NEW HOUSE

There are species of termites, or white ants, in the tropical countries that build themselves strong nests of clay, often twenty feet or more high and as much across. Such a nest, when abandoned by its builders, can shelter a man from wind and rain.

White ants build nests several
yards high (Australia)

There are several types of carnivorous plants that trap and devour insects. One of these is the swamp-dwelling sundew. When an insect settles on the sundew's viscous leaf, the leaf instantly contracts. When the victim has been squeezed dry the leaf opens up, ready for a new meal.

In the forests of Australia, great colonies of luminescent toadstools spring up in the spring and autumn. The light they emit is sufficient for reading. In Brazil there is a huge toadstool known as the Veiled Lady, which in something like two hours grows to a height of a foot and a half. This mushroom glows a bright green by night, and the fireflies gather to dance around it. The mycelium of the ordinary honey agaric also glows by night.

The emperor boa, found in Brazil and Venezuela, is a very handsome snake, growing to a length of thirteen feet. Young boas of this breed are often kept in barns and warehouses, and even in private homes, for their skill in catching rats. They become so accustomed to their homes that, if removed, they almost always find their way back. When a house is sold, therefore, its boa is generally sold with it.

The flying dogs and flying foxes of India, Australia, and New Guinea are large fruit-eating bats which plunder the orchards by

◁ A carnivorous plant devouring its prey

A flying dog (Seychelles Islands)

night, devouring mangos, bananas, and figs. In the daytime they sleep, suspending themselves head down from some convenient branch.

There are bats in the tropics which live on the blood of birds and animals, wild or domestic. They attack even sleeping humans, puncturing the skin and licking the blood that oozes out.


## THE CRANE-HERD

Cranes were once plentiful in North America. But that was long ago. With the passing years, more and more land was ploughed up, more and more swamps drained; more and more of the birds killed by sportsmen, and more and more of their nests plundered of eggs. And a time came when only a few score cranes remained alive.

Nowadays, America's cranes are under constant supervision. When the one remaining flock takes flight from Canada's marshy plains to its winter home in southern Texas and Louisiana, the birds are followed by a special convoy plane. This protection will continue until the cranes have multiplied sufficiently to be out of danger of extinction.

America has known not only bird herders, but even bird sentinels.

When in 1907 predacious shooting had left only one last nest of eider ducks in the Gulf of Maine, a sentinel had to be set by the nest to save these valuable birds from complete extinction.


## WOODEN COWS

In several of the Latin American countries one comes upon groves of tall, straight trees, with smooth bark and glossy leathery leaves. These trees bear a berry-like fruit; but it is not for the fruit that they are cultivated. Cow trees, they are called, or milk trees. When their bark notched, a thick white fluid begins to run. In one "milking" a cow tree may yield three or even four quarts of this fluid, which in both taste and chemical make-up is very similar to ordinary cow's milk. There is a hint of bitterness, true, but this disappears if the milk is slightly diluted with water and brought to a boil.

The papaya, or melon tree (Australia)

Other interesting trees of the tropics are the bread-fruit tree and the sausage tree. The breadfruit, when baked, resembles bread, and makes good eating. The fruit of the sausage tree, however, though it looks very much like liver sausages, is inedible.

## BIRD MILK

No bird on earth has mammary glands; and it is only mammary glands that produce milk. Yet bird milk exists.

For eighteen days after hatching, the young of the domestic pigeon are fed on partly digested food regurgitated from their parents' crops—a white, semi-liquid mass known as pigeon's milk.

The young of the emperor penguin, away down in the Antarctic, are similarly fed.

Bird milk far excels cow's milk in both fat content and nutrition value. Whale milk, too, is very nourishing. It is twelve times as rich as cow's milk in fat content.

## A SINECURE

What won't a man do, if he lives by burgling, to get into other men's houses? In India, burglars often resort to the assistance of the varan, or monitor lizard, to help them up a wall. The monitor is a large, strong-limbed lizard, sometimes over six feet long. The burglar ties a rope around its middle and sends it up the wall. As soon as the lizard finds a chink or crack that suits its fancy, it will take shelter there, clinging so tight that the burglar can safely climb the rope and reach the roof or windows of the house.

But it is not only burglars that make use of reptiles.

In Australia, snakes are often trained to safeguard shops against theft. When a shop is shut up for the night, the snake is let out of its box. Should a thief enter, the snake will promptly wind itself around his legs, generally frightening him so that he shouts for help and is only too pleased when the police arrive.

Feeding time for the young of
the emperor penguins, down in
the Antarctic

## INCENDIARY

After a disastrous forest fire in India, all efforts to trace out the culprit were long unsuccessful. In the end, however, it was clearly established that the fire had been started by a flower.

Yes, a flower, no more and no less. A flower whose stalk and leaves are so saturated with inflammable oils that in dry, hot weather they are liable to burst into flame.

In the Soviet Union, in the Tien Shan mountains, there is a plant called the burning bush, the leaves of which contain ether in such quantities that in hot, dry weather they sometimes blaze up, and may cause serious forest fires.


## BIRDHOUSE SEEDS

It occurred to someone at the Ascania-Nova reserve (U.S.S.R.) that there was no need to build birdhouses out of boards, when empty gourds could serve the purpose. When cleaned out and dried the lagenaria or bottle gourd, makes a very convenient and durable house. All it lacks is an entrance, and that is easily made.

Put to the test, the idea proved a good one. Not only starlings and titmice, but flycatchers, sparrows, and even jackdaws built their nests in the gourd birdhouses.

They now hang on many trees, these houses—not human handiwork, but the product of the soil.


## DUCKSHOT

Ducks, like chickens, have the habit of swallowing coarse sand, or even pebbles, to grind the rough food that they eat, and thus help in its digestion. Often, lead birdshot is found in a duck's craw—swallowed either as a substitute for sand, or because it resembles the seeds of the pond weed, on which ducks feed.

# DIGGING FOR FISH

In India, fish is caught even in time of drought, when the rivers all run dry. For lack of water, of course, fishing rods are left at home. Spades are more useful, inasmuch as the fish lie underground, and require not so much to be hooked as to be dug up.

The climbing fish (*Anabas scandens*), found in Indian rivers, can crawl over stony or grassy ground, and is said even to climb trees. When its river goes dry, this fish crawls overland to the nearest fresh water or, if there is no water near, buries itself in the mud. Here it makes easy prey for fishers armed with spades.

The protopterus, an African fish, buries itself in the river mud in the dry season, curling up so that its tail protects its head and covering itself with a slime which, combined with mud and sand, forms a crust that prevents loss of moisture. When the rainy season sets in the water dissolves this crust and the fish is free to swim again.

In the Soviet Union, too, there is a fish—the loach—which is caught by digging in wet river mud or in half-dried-out streams.

## MERRY RICE

Scientists in India declare that music may be made to affect the rate of growth of plants. Experimenting with various sounds, they have succeeded in accelerating or retarding plant growth, particularly in rice and in tobacco.

Carnations are very sensitive to noise. Set beside a loudspeaker, they soon begin to droop.

## CUMBERSOME MONEY

Outside every house on Yap Island, in the Carolines, stand huge stone wheels, very much like millstones. They are not millstones, however. They are money. These "coins", some of them as much as eight feet in diameter and something like a ton in weight, are rolled about at need with the aid of a strong bamboo rod.

This stone money is used only by men. The women of the island have money of their own, in the form of bamboo mats and nacre shells.

In Russia, in 1725, there was an issue of copper coins in the shape of slabs. A coin worth one ruble weighed three and a half pounds; a coin worth fifty kopeks, a pound and three-quarters, and a ten-kopek piece, a little over a third of a pound. These coins were very heavy and inconvenient, and were replaced two years later by an issue of round coins of smaller size and weight, the new five-kopek pieces weighing only about seven ounces.

## BING-BANG, THE HUNTER

### Dog Powder

Can a dog's sense of smell be intensified? It can. A stimulant known as phenamin, administered in doses of 0.15 to 0.30 grains, has been found to double this sense. Under the influence of this drug dogs have kept to a hare's trail three times as long as normally, very seldom losing the scent.

### Old Man Mazai and the Elephants

Floods are often disastrous to the animal world.

When the African river Zambezi was dammed, in 1959, it overflowed its banks and flooded all the country round.

**The service seems to satisfy**

▽

△
Life-saving during a flood
(Africa)

The forest beasts sought shelter on every elevation. The local nature protection society called on the population for help. Boats and rafts were made ready, and hundreds of arrows were prepared, smeared with soporifics and sedatives. These arrows, shot at lions, leopards, antelopes, or buffalo, put the animals to sleep and made it possible to load them onto boats or rafts and bring them to safety. The rhinos, however, were so thick-skinned that the arrows could not affect them; and they were too heavy, in any case, to be loaded onto any sort of craft. They had to be simply driven into the water and made to swim to shore.

144

## Herbivorous Wolves

Collective-farm night watchmen have often noticed wolves in the melon patches by night, gorging themselves on ripe melons. In the winter months, hungry wolves have been seen in the turnip fields, digging out roots that the harvesters have missed. They are known, too, to eat many sorts of berries.

In zoological gardens antelopes—those most peaceable and herbivorous of creatures—have been seen to kill and eat birds. Arctic explorers report that reindeer, in the spring, often kill and eat lemmings, and also plunder birds' nests, devouring both eggs and young.

This is believed to be caused by an insufficiency of albumen and minerals in the animals' diet.

## A Gigantic Nest

The largest known bird nests are those of the brush turkeys, or mound birds. The brush turkeys do not sit on their eggs. They scrape together great mounds of sand, grass, and fallen leaves, and lay their eggs inside these

**Brush turkeys do not sit on their eggs**
▽

mounds, where the heat generated by decay keeps the eggs warm and eventually hatches them. Sometimes several birds will build a nest together, and all lay their eggs in it—fifty or sixty.

The nests of the brush turkey are sometimes very large—over twenty feet high, and as much as two hundred tons in weight. It would take seventy three-ton trucks to cart one of them to a museum.

The mound birds have also been known to lay their eggs in the warm ashes around the crater of an active volcano.

Sea water has no monopoly of salts. There are salts in rain, and snow, and hoarfrost, and hail. There are salts in clouds, and also in fogs. There is salt in tears, and particularly in the tears of the crocodile. In fact, it has recently been demonstrated that a crocodile's tears are simply its way of discarding surplus salts that have accumulated in its system.

There is an animal in South America called the sloth, an indolent, slow-moving creature. The sloth is greyish brown in colour, but it looks green, because every hair on its body is encased, as in a sheath, with microscopic algae that live on the sloth's sweat and on the carbon dioxide that it exhales. Moss-grown in this way, the sloth is so like the foliage around it that it cannot be easily detected.

## A Pointer Pig

Good to eat, like mushrooms, but growing underground, with neither stalk nor cap—this is a fungus known as the truffle. About the size of your fist, and the shape of a potato. It makes very good eating, once it's found; but the finding of it isn't simple. And so people often train pigs to help them. Pigs have a keen sense of smell, and are very fond of truffles. The hunter takes his trained pig to the woods with him, the pig finds the truffles, and all the hunter has to do is dig them up.

Not only pigs, but dogs, and even tame bears, may be taught to hunt truffles. Some dogs will point at truffles as they do at game.

## SAILOR TOPMAST'S TALES

Sailors, like hunters, often get into the most amazing adventures.

The steamer *Kuban*, one day, got into a storm in the Pacific. A great wave caught up one of the crew, seaman Alexander P., and washed him overboard. But the next wave caught him up again and threw him back on deck.

In the Antarctic Ocean, in 1927, a floating iceberg was sighted that proved to be 112 miles long. The portion of an iceberg that projects above the water is sometimes over 200 feet high. An iceberg's "life span" averages about ten years. Icebergs have been encountered as far north as the Tropic of Capricorn.

Fish have often been known to attack ships.

In 1945 the tanker *Barbara* was attacked by a swordfish, which pierced the steel plating in two places. The crew succeeded in getting a noose

10*

⊐ A swordfish

A huge iceberg in the Antarctic.
Beside it, the Soviet ship *Ob*
▽

△
A bridge iceberg along the coast
of Greenland

on the tail of this fish, and dragged it on board. It was twenty-two feet long, and weighed fourteen hundred pounds. Its speed in the water was over forty miles an hour.

In 1944, along the coast of Africa, a swordfish thrust its snout through a fishing boat and pulled it down into the sea, leaving the crew afloat in the water.

Not long ago, again, a swordfish attacked the British warship *Leopold* and pierced it in several places. Water flooded the hold, and divers had to be sent down to patch the leaks.

### Fish Catch Fish

Every autumn shoals of a fish called taiyu enter bays and river mouths along the coast of the South China Sea to spawn. Anglers have found that the best bait for this fish is the tail of one of its kin. When one fish has been hooked, another will often catch at its tail. A third may seize the tail of the second, and so on, until as many as six hang from the one hook, each succeeding fish larger than the one before.

Fish are neither deaf nor mute. They may be located and identified by the sounds that they emit. Malayan fishers eavesdrop upon them, ducking their heads into the water to determine what sort of fish are about, and in what number, and what they are doing.

The jufili, for instance, when they are feeding, make sounds that resemble the crackling of rice in a frying pan. The gourami, an aquarium fish, makes sounds like the quiet tapping of wooden spoons. Drumfish communicate with one another in words that sound like "tuk, tuk". The "voice" of the herring resembles the chirping of sparrows, and that of the sprat is like a dull drone. Thus, each fish has its own way of speaking.

## IN THE BELLY OF A WHALE

In September 1958 a Canadian magazine reproduced an excerpt from an old and little-known book about the perils and profits of whaling. The excerpt described an encounter with a cachalot that took place in 1891.

The ship that sighted this cachalot sent out a boat with eight men at the oars. When the boat got close enough the men shot two harpoons. Both lodged in the whale's flank. In its fury, the wounded beast upset the boat. A rescuing party succeeded in saving only six of the men. The seventh was dead, and the eighth—James Bartley—was not to be found.

The whale was killed and brought on deck. Working over its carcass, the men noticed a stirring in the stomach. And inside the stomach, when they had laid it open, they found their missing mate, James Bartley—unconscious, but alive.

For many weeks, in a hospital on the coast, doctors fought for Bartley's life. At length he came to himself and was able to tell his story. When the whale upset the boat Bartley had been thrown up into the air, and coming down he had landed in the whale's open mouth. Only later, in the whale's stomach, had he lost consciousness.

Bartley's health was badly shaken. His face, neck, and arms were covered with white spots, where the whale's gastric juice had begun its action.

He went to sea again, however, shipping on a small boat, and sailed for five years more. In 1896 he died.

The predacious cachalot, unlike other whales, has a very wide throat. Whole sharks, six and even nine feet long, have repeatedly been found in the stomachs of captured cachalots. In chief, however, their food consists of octopi and calamaries, to find which the whale dives, sometimes, to depths of half a mile and more.

The remnants of deepwater fish and calamaries found in the stomachs of cachalots emit a strong, bluish phosphorescent light, issuing chiefly from the bodies, eyes, and beaks of the calamaries and from the bones of the fish.

It is thought that this light is caused by the dissolution in the whale's gastric juice of the photophores, or light-emitting organs, of its victims.

## The Size of Waves

Waves of enormous size sometimes rise in the ocean. Largest of all are those caused by earthquakes or by the eruption of underwater volcanos. Tsunami, such waves are called. They attain a height of a hundred and sixty feet, and a velocity of 450 miles an hour. They are sometimes 125 miles long.

This ship was wrecked by a huge wave
▽

Tsunami waves carry desolation and death. In 1896 seven such waves, in the course of a few minutes, killed twenty-seven thousand people and injured five thousand more. They are capable of throwing a ship far inland.

## THE DIVER'S TALES

### Green Blood

Captain Cousteau, the well-known diver, harpooned a shark, one day, at a considerable depth, and was amazed to see that the blood flowing from the wound was coloured green.

In deep water all bright colours—red, orange, yellow—lose their brilliance and turn a muddy green. Even blood, deep underwater, looks green.

That, of course, is simply an optical illusion. Some types of blood, however, are really green.

The blood of vertebrates is red because of the iron that enters into the composition of its haemoglobin. But there are a number of sea worms that have chlorocruorin in their blood in place of haemoglobin; and inasmuch as chlorocruorin contains iron oxide, the blood of these worms is green. The blood of crayfish, spiders, scorpions, octopi, and cuttlefish is blue, because there is copper in the haemacyanin which takes the place of haemoglobin in their blood.

Thus, not all blood is red. Some blood is green, and some is blue.

### Red Tide

In October 1955 strange red waves began to roll up on the coast of the Gulf of Mexico. Every living creature that got into this fearful red water was instantly killed. The red waves threw onto the shore thousands upon thousands of dead fish, crabs, mollusks, littering the coast over a stretch of more than 230 miles. The red tide flowed for thirteen days.

All work in the ports had to be stopped, because the stench of the decaying fish affected the workers' throats and eyes.

Similar calamities have occurred on the coasts of Peru and California, of Africa and Japan.

Some scientists attribute these red tides to the presence of myriads of microscopic red cells in the water. Normally, no more than a thousand of these poisonous cells can be found in a quart of sea water. During the "red tide", there are over sixty million to a quart.

### Dolphins Play Ball

There is a huge aquarium in the United States in which captive dolphins often play basketball. They are very skilful at catching the ball on their snouts and throwing it up so that it will fall through the basket. On the bank, an audience of seals roars encouragement, and claps its flippers in applause.

Dolphins can jump through a hoop, and "sing" duets. Leaping high out of the water, they catch food straight from the hands of visitors.

In pursuit of fish, dol- ▷ phins often leap up out of the water. Trainers have further developed this trait

## At the Bottom of the Sea

All sorts of fearful tales are told about the giant clam, the largest known mollusk. Its shell is often five feet in diameter, and weighs 450 to 550 pounds. This clam lies hidden in silt and seaweed, only the rims of its half-open shell projecting above the surface of the sea bottom. Should a diver have the

Hans Hass tried in vain to force open the shell of the giant clam
▽

△
**The devil fish**

evil luck to touch it with foot or hand, it will snap shut and the diver will never rise.

Hans Hass, underwater explorer, once poked a giant clam with an artificial leg. The shell shut instantly, and held firm as a steel trap. Hass tried for half an hour to free the leg. He did not succeed.

In the Red Sea one may watch the dance of the devil fish—a gigantic ray with a pair of movable appendages on its head somewhat resembling a pair of horns. The devil fish is sometimes twenty feet wide, and it may weigh a ton. For all that, it is capable of leaping as much as ten feet out of the water.

The arctic medusa, a large jellyfish found in the northern seas, measures over six feet across its disc, and the length of its tentacles is sixty to a hundred feet. It emits a greenish glow.

In a California aquarium a female octopus known as Mephista brooded its eggs in a basket formed of its own tentacles, caring for them tenderly until they hatched.

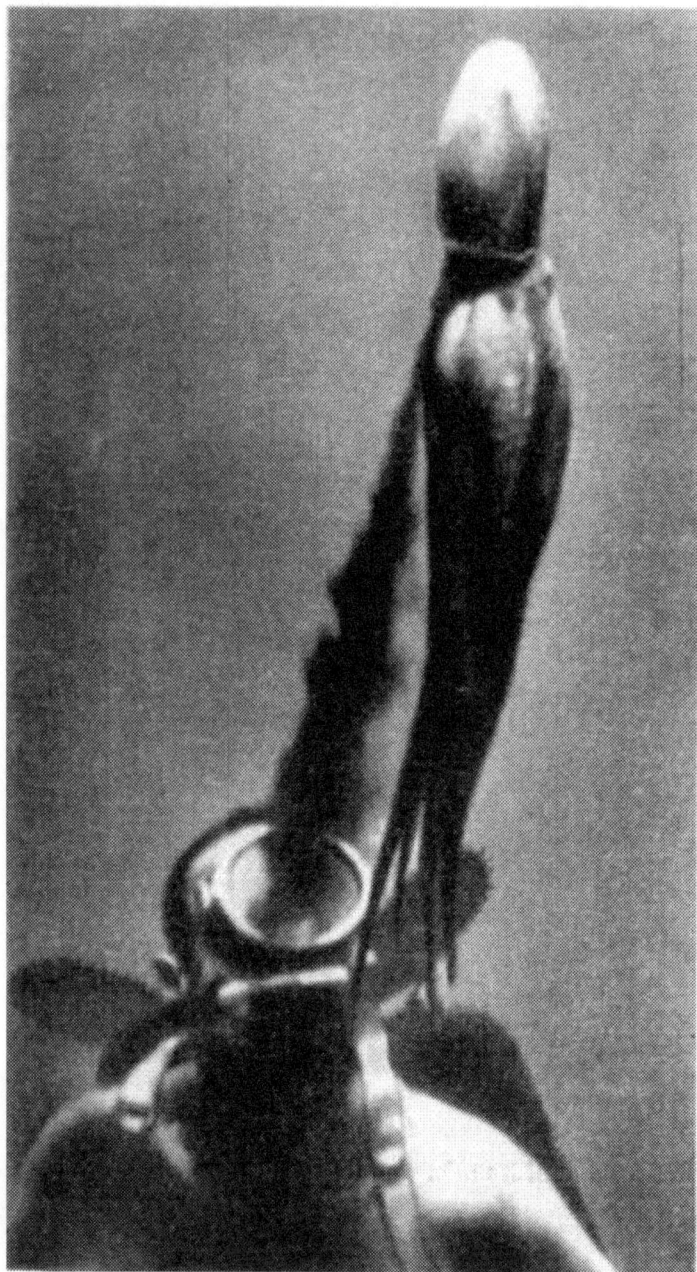

◁ Cuttlefish shoot through the sea on the principle of jet aircraft

Δ

A captured calamary

There is a tropical perch which has formed a rather unusual habit. When danger threatens, the mother perch gathers its young into its mouth and carries them to safety.

Certain fishes—the electric rays, the electric eels, the electric catfish—are equipped with special organs that can produce a strong electric charge, useful both in defence and in attack.

Cuttlefish, calamaries, and octopi shoot through the sea on the principle of jet aircraft, pumping water through themselves. The calamary gets up such speed that it can leap high into the air.

## MY FRIEND MAGMA, THE GEOLOGIST

### A Musical Mountain

There are "musical" mountains in many countries. On a sunny day, or in a gusty wind, these mountains produce sounds reminiscent of music —sometimes clear and ringing, sometimes blaring, sometimes soft and soothing. You seem to distinguish separate instruments—flutes, violins, sometimes an organ. When trod upon, the sand may seem to bark like a dog, or it may twang like a taut string.

The superstitious tell tales of sirens that lure travellers into the desert, or of bells ringing in ancient cities long buried beneath the sands.

In the Chinese province of Kansu there was once a sand hill about five hundred feet high. Once every year, during the feast of the dragon, people would climb this hill and go sliding down its slopes; and the hill would rumble and roar like genuine thunder.

The dwellers of Thunwang (city of the sands), in the Lob Nor desert, were warned of approaching sand storms by a nearby sand mountain, which would begin to rumble, long before the storm arrived, as though someone inside it were beating huge drums.

In the Soviet Union, too, there are several such "musical" mountains.

What makes the mountains musical is not yet known, though scientists have suggested a number of possible explanations.

These sand hills sing
▽

## Flowers That Talk

There are many plants that will grow only on soils of definite chemical make-up, so that they have come to be known as indicators of the minerals they choose to live with. The lead plant, in America, is so known because it grows in places where there are deposits of lead ore. In Belgium, outcrops of zinc ore are invariably marked by a plant known as the Galmei violet. In Bohemia, the starflower grows only on tin mine dumps. In the U.S.S.R., the larger varieties of kokpek indicate oil, and gypsophila grows along veins of copper ore. Pasque-flower, when growing over nickel deposits, changes in shape and in the colour of its petals. It has been noticed, too, that copper shavings, when put into the soil beneath a rose bush, turn the roses blue. Thus, flowers speak to us, showing us where to seek mineral treasure.

## AN ETERNAL STEW

In 1949 live crucian carp were found in the Goryachinsky hot spring, near Lake Baikal. The fish showed no sign of discomfort, although the temperature of the water was 107°F.

The hot springs of California are inhabited by another fish of the carp family, which seems perfectly happy at a temperature of 126°F.

## A BIRD THAT EATS NAILS

On cutting open an ostrich, one day, its owners found in its stomach over nine pounds of variegated junk: rags, sand, three lumps of iron, nine copper coins, a copper hinge, two iron keys, seventeen copper nails, twelve iron nails, several balls of lead, buttons, bells, etc., etc. For all this dead weight in its insides, the bird had been healthy and well-fed, and had shown no signs of discomfort.

Pellets of undigested matter cast up by a crow were found to contain: coal, cinders, bits of broken brick, tea leaves, glass, lime, bits of leather strapping, bits of plastic, metal foil, an indiarubber eraser, chips of wood and bark, paper, thread, hair, eggshells, cellophane, and cotton fluff.

Neither the ostrich nor the crow, of course, feeds on nails or glass. Some of these articles are swallowed by chance, together with the food that the birds eat. Others are swallowed deliberately, to grind up the food in the birds' stomachs.

## A GREAT FEAST

Every people has its own national dishes.

What one people eats with relish, to another may seem outlandish—to say the least.

The Chinese, for instance, are very fond of bird's nest soup. The nests of which this soup is made—those of the salangane, or of other small swifts of similar habits—are composed chiefly of the dried glutinous secretions of the birds' salivary glands.

In the market places of the Antilles Islands, you can buy dried locusts. In the Sudan, you will be offered various

50,000 portions of fish in one frying pan
▽

The feast of the fish in the little town of Camogli (Italy)

dishes made of termites and of caterpillars.

A portion of termites, incidentally, contains more than four times the amount of calories found in an equal portion of beef.

The people of Libya dry locusts in the sun, grind them into flour, and bake cakes out of the flour.

Restaurants in the United States serve a salad made of nasturtium buds, and also a nasturtium sauce.

Birds' nests, young bee larvae, and white ants are eaten on the island of Java.

In China, besides bird's nest soup, you may be offered dried shark fins, dried frogs, cuttlefish and their eggs, a salad of young bamboo sprouts, or a dish of trepang or sea slugs.

Certain species of frogs and snails are eaten in France.

Snails contain 20 times as much vitamin C as the best butter.

They are eaten with red wine, or with cheese, or in soups or omelettes. These dishes are the pride of the French cuisine.

In some countries snakes are eaten, and worms, and grubs.

A Parisian café once organised a public tasting of a pie filled with May bug larvae. All who tasted pronounced the pie excellent, and some even asked for second portions.

At the yearly feast of the fish in the little Italian town of Camogli a huge frying pan, fifteen feet across, is set up in the town square, and fish is fried in it—50,000 portions at a time.

Fifty thousand portions constitute five tons of fish, and 260 gallons of olive oil go into the frying.

## MONUMENT TO A BUG

◁ Monument to the cotton boll weevil (Enterprise, Alabama, U.S.A.)

In the state of Alabama, U.S.A., a monument has been erected to the cotton boll weevil, with an inscription expressing gratitude for the prosperity this bug has brought the citizens of the town of Enterprise.

Some time ago the boll weevil wrought such damage in the cotton fields that the farmers were compelled to shift to other crops; and these unexpectedly turned out to be far more profitable than cotton.

In the Australian town of Burnarga a monument has been erected to a caterpillar.

Back in the nineteenth century, a cactus known as opuntia was

Before the caterpillar came to
the rescue (Australia)
▽

△
Three years after

imported into Australia. The opuntia blossoms handsomely, and many farmers used it to hedge their fields. It was not long, however, before the new hedge got out of control and began to overrun the country. Then the farmers began to fight it—chopping down the cacti, rooting them up, setting fire to them. All effort was in vain. The opuntia continued to spread. Finally a caterpillar, the larva of the cactoblastis, was brought in from South America. In ten years this caterpillar cleared all the fields of the "rabid" cactus. The grateful farmers had a monument set up to it.

## THE GOLDEN FISH

A circular issued by the Japanese Ministry of Agriculture calls upon the residents of districts often troubled by earthquake to breed a certain small white fish in their aquariums. It has been noticed that this fish becomes very restless before earthquakes, thus giving the people warning several hours ahead.

Earthquakes are frequent in Japan, occurring, in one district or another, from three to five times a year; so that this little fish's gift of prophecy makes it truly a golden fish to the Japanese.

There are fish, too, that foretell the weather.

In some parts of China, the loach serves as such a barometer. It grows restless before cloudy weather, and races desperately about its aquarium when it is going to rain. Only in three or four cases out of a hundred, it is said, are these forecasts mistaken.

## CLAP THE WHALE ON ITS BACK

Crown Prince Gustav Strait, dividing James Ross Island from Graham Land, once froze over unexpectedly and barred the road to the open sea for a school of whales. To breathe, the whales were compelled to thrust their heads up through holes in the ice.

The members of a British Antarctic expedition were able to clap the whales on their backs.

Snow is sometimes red, or blue, or green, or even black. The colouring is caused by microscopic algae.

One day in 1959 black snow came down for four hours on end on the southern slopes of the Caucasus Mountains. It covered the white snow on the mountain sides with a two-inch layer of black. Meteorologists ascribed the black snow to dust, soot, and ashes carried by the wind from Baku, Kishli, and Sumgait.

* * *

The editor laid down the grey copybook and looked up at Paramon, with a queer glint in his eyes. Then he got up and went over to the window. The April night was dark, but the world that lay so still in the darkness was very much alive. Its breath came softly in at the window. It was full of wonder and mystery, this world; crisscrossed with endless roads that called imperatively to the imagination.

"It's April first," the editor said.

"The world's most truthful day," Paramon responded.

"Incidentally, Paramon," the editor asked, "do you know what your name means?"

"Of course I do," Paramon responded. "Reliable, it means, and Firm."

When a whale can be clapped on its back

"Good day to you," the editor said.

"Till we meet again," Paramon responded.

▽

www.ingramcontent.com/pod-product-compliance
Lightning Source LLC
Chambersburg PA
CBHW021158010426
R18062100001B/R180621PG41931CBX00021B/37